DAVID!! :)

go with go CRAZY go TOTALLY NUTS

MURRAY

2015

NUTTER'S PLAYGROUND!
BE AFRAID... BE VERY AFRAID

NUTS!AB

the nutter experience

UT FOOD

not just a meal but an adventure

FOREWORD BY BRIAN TURNER CBE

When I first met Andrew (not many of us call him that, well, his mum and I do) I wasn't over-impressed by his inability either to stand still or to put away the copious amounts of alcohol that most of us took for granted, nor his style of cooking.

It's amazing how time changes lots of things isn't it? About four years ago, Nutter (see even that's changed) was included on the cast list of chefs taking part in the Weakest Link.

He's never forgiven me for making sure that he was the first to depart. Especially as Anne Robinson, yes, that lady, seemed to have an eye for him! I seem to remember the lads from Ready Steady Cook, myself included, had decided he should go first as he wasn't really part of our team, and well, the shirt he had on that day was so Nutter, he just had to go! Andrew was convinced I hated him. Not true of course, it just had to be the way it was that day.

Since then, our paths have crossed frequently, with the delicious and precocious Jenni Barnett on the much-missed show Good Food Live and more so on our trips to Cape Town and Johannesburg for the Good Food and Wine Shows. Boy, could I tell you some stories.

Nutter (let's stick with that now) has shown me that he is a skilled and inventive cook and that he has a huge passion for our industry. He never does anything (and I mean anything) by half, giving his time and talent to whatever project he is on.

This book definitely reflects his personality and his drive but, more than that, shows us all what a clever and sincere cook he is. I'm sure you will enjoy reading it but even more, I'm sure you will love cooking and eating the food.

Brian Turner CBE

"Nutter has shown me that he is a skilled and inventive cook and that he has a huge passion for our industry

Text:	Andrew Nutter
Edited by:	Martin Edwards, Chris Brierley
Design:	Paul Cocker, Richard Abbey, Heather Pass, Dan Wray
Photography:	Tim Bradley
Additional photography:	Matthew Stansfield
First published in 2009 on behalf of:	Andrew Nutter, Nutters Restaurant www.nuttersrestaurant.co.uk (01706) 650167
Published by:	Regional Magazine Company Limited www.regionalmagazine.co.uk (0114) 2506300
Printed and bound in Great Britain by:	Butler Tanner & Dennis Ltd.

RMC BOOKS

GREAT BRITISH BOOKS
PRODUCED & PRINTED IN THE UK

CONTENTS

DEDICATIONS & ACKNOWLEDGEMENTS

With grateful thanks to all of the following for their help in creating this book:

The Rochdale Observer/MEN Media
for their kind permission to use Tim Bradley's work, as a result of which
our nominated charity Spring Hill Hospice benefitted.

All the staff at Nutters
for their continuing hard work and determination to maintain our place as one of the North-west's finest

My reception team - Louise and Phoebe
the queens of the email system, who managed to decipher recipes from my spidery handwriting

Dave, my restaurant manager,
a cracking bloke, who puts up with all my tantrums, usually with his catchphrase 'Deal with it!'

My suppliers and producers,
who supply me with the finest produce. Having the best at hand makes my life easier.

Martin Edwards
for his skills in editing my scribbles and in helping reflect my character in this book

Paul Cocker
for having a surname almost as bad as mine, but also for his design genius which helped realise my vision

Tim Bradley
for the amazing photography

My parents Jean and Rodney
who work so hard on a day-to-day basis to maintain the standards of the restaurant.

My core team of chefs - Carl, Pilky, Big Ads, Ben, Steve - also Nick, Adam and Jason
for their tireless support in my never-ending quest to push out the boundaries of
what can be achieved in the kitchen

To mum and dad,
Jean and Rodney for
their endless support and
hard work, without
whom Nutters would not
be what it is today

ABOUT THE AUTHOR

A ndrew Nutter is one of the most exciting and innovative of the new breed of celebrity chefs to hit the culinary circuit.

At 16 he trained at London's Savoy Hotel, followed by stints at Michelin starred restaurants in France. He opened his restaurant Nutters, near Rochdale, Greater Manchester aged 21 to great acclaim, winning North-west Chef of The Year, UK Restaurant of The Year and a recent Outstanding Achievement Award.

His media career spans his own series Utter Nutter Remote Control Cooking and The Flying Chef through to shows on ITV and the BBC, including Ready Steady Cook, This Morning and GMTV.

Nutter remains at the forefront of modern British cuisine, not only here in the UK where he works alongside the major supermarkets, endorsing and promoting local products, but also abroad, linked mainly to South Africa, where he regularly demonstrates and America where some of his shows are broadcast. His first book Utter Nutter has globally sold out.

THE PHOTOGRAPHER

After discovering a passion for photography from his grandfather as a child, Tim Bradley took it up first as a hobby, then later as a career.

He studied photography at Leeds Polytechnic, then went straight into a job on the Accrington Observer. After gaining further experience at the Rochdale Observer he joined the Guardian Media Newspaper Group, covering a range of work from the Commonwealth Games in Manchester to food photography.

As well as his role as Deputy Picture Editor for the Manchester Evening News/Guardian - MEN Media, he is a noted freelance - photographing everything from weddings and portraits to the food created by chef Andrew Nutter.

He was named Press Gazette Photographer of the Year 2009, and O2 Media Awards Photographer of the Year in Greater Manchester and Lancashire.

www.timbradleyphotography.com

NUTS ABOUT LIFE

I may be the clown prince in my kingdom of Rochdale, according to one journalist. But I'm totally serious about food. It's the only way to be. When you decide to devote your life to something, you're not doing it for a laugh – although there have been plenty of lighter moments in even the grandest of kitchens along the way.

For me, the decision was made early. I learned the basics of home cooking from my mother at a young age, and me and two sisters Suzanne and Gillian used to take it in turns to cook the Sunday tea. Every so often we'd have a go at cookery competitions in newspapers and magazines and before long, the prizes were rolling in, be they trips to America, televisions or cookers.

When a mere lad of 15, I suddenly found myself contending for the title of Daily Mail Cook of the Year. This time I was up against adults and Anton Edelmann, the maître chef de cuisine at The Savoy Hotel, was one of the judges. He came over after we'd finished and asked what my plans were after I left school. Not sure, came the response.

The awards were presented, but then Anton rose to his feet and at a stroke changed my life. There and then, he offered me an apprenticeship at The Savoy after I left school. And so at the age of 16 my bags were packed and I waved Manchester goodbye for the big world of London.

After paying rent at my lodgings I had £15 a week left to live on. This was the ladder of life and I was on the first step.

I'll never forget the first day at The Savoy. So this was a professional kitchen at the very top of the pecking order – 80 chefs running round, some screaming, lots shouting and all orders being read out in French by the sous chefs. My school French had stopped at "Quelle heure est-il?", so this was going to be a challenge.

THE ENGLISHMAN ABROAD

On yer bike... with the motorcycling fraternity while in town for the food festival, Johannesburg

Cape Town 2007

Durban 2008 – By the sea with fellow chefs Reza Mahammad, Ben O'Donoghue, Patrick Williams and Brian Turner

It was an experience like no other. I met some wonderful characters along the way and some chefs who have gone on to great things. Marcus Wareing started the same day as me, Giorgio Locatelli was my sous chef and Andy Needham ruled the veg station. Richard Phillips was the starter king, Gary Durrent chef tournant and who could forget premier sous chef David Sharland? All have made their mark thanks to the sheer grounding and understanding of food that Anton Edelmann drilled into us all.

After 3 years of intensive training the time had come to take the leap across the channel to France. After stints at the Chateau De Remaisnil and Hotel Berangere in the Alps I settled for a year at the Chateau De Montreuil. I loved the town, the people, the mere way of life. And this time, it was the whole kitchen, not just the sous chefs, who spoke French. Mon Dieu!

After a spell working with Gary Rhodes, a job offer came to open a restaurant in Montreuil. I eagerly rang my parents to tell them the news. Instead of the enthusiastic response I expected, there was an ominous request – "before you do anything, come back up north for the weekend". So it was that I returned to Lancashire and my dad revealed my future. He had found a suitable site for a restaurant. Not only that, family members were ready to chip in and the opportunity for me to prove myself on home turf had come. I couldn't say no.

And so French Connection opened. We never advertised and let word of mouth speak for us. Manchester Evening News food critic Ray King named us his Restaurant of the Year and described my cooking as 'a touch of magic.' I never looked back.

More awards came, with publicity in their wake. On one occasion, on winning Lancashire Life Chef of the Year, I turned up with Nutter shaved in the back of my head. The media took the bait and I was soon plastered all over the magazines. TV companies picked up on my youthful eccentricities and the next minute with a whirlwind of agents, managers and hype, I was the next big thing. Previous identity discarded, I became Nutter in the eyes of the media, so the restaurant changed its name and Nutters was born.

I was all of a sudden the main attraction in an interactive lifestyle show, Afternoon Live on ITV, co-hosting with Bibi Baskin, David Emanuel and my Mancunian side-kick Melanie Sykes. The show went out three times a week live from London and we cooked via a satellite link. It was very groundbreaking at the time and certainly didn't do me or the restaurant any harm.

Channel 5 quickly signed me up and me, Nancy Lam and the Spice Girls helped launch the channel. My show on 5 was Utter Nutter, a radical cookery show where I shared my love of food with passion, fireworks and flames, returning each day to cook in the restaurant. Over the next few years I did Ready Steady Cook, was resident chef with Lorraine on GMTV, and Granada's resident chef with Lucy Meacock. With 10 years in the media spotlight behind me, the restaurant was bulging at its seams. Word reached us that Wolstenholme Manor, dating back to 1850, was up for sale. A deal was done and before we knew it the restaurant moved 2 miles down the road to its present home.

Its 6½ acres of groomed park land, panoramic views, its gothic arches and sumptuous surroundings providing the ideal backdrop for Nutters cuisine.

Where it all started. Me as a lad and my two sisters on our first TV show

Kids KAFE

Now what do I do with this?

So that's my story. Sitting here writing this, I reflect on the time when I first started out... those early mornings going to market at 4.00am, working all day and night, and for £92 a week... is it worth it? Never for a minute have I doubted it. That's why I'm serious about food. It's my life.

They don't come fresher than this. On a fishing trip with the chefs, Bridlington

...AND AT HOME

Adam gets down to basics in the kitchen at Nutters

...deal with this ...h Dave, our ...manager

Pilky demonstrates his preparation skills

Look like you own the place, the photographer said. Didn't know you had bouncers guarding the door, said everyone else

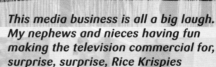

Louise, bless her, the angelic public face of Nutters, taking a table reservation

This media business is all a big laugh. My nephews and nieces having fun making the television commercial for, surprise, surprise, Rice Krispies

UNDER THE MEDIA SPOTLIGHT

So the producer says to me "Nutter, go and stick your head in a crate of tomatoes". Do I reply;

a) I am a serious chef and I will not stoop to such cheap stunts?

b) Take one. Action?

Filming a demo at the Chelsea Flower Show

With Heston Blumenthal at the Good Food Guide Awards 2010

THE GOOD FOOD GUIDE

Chef buys one of first Z3s to appear in the UK. Chef turns Z3 upside down and wrecks it on Christmas Eve. Result; headlines in national newspapers, Utter Nutter ratings soar

Sure, I did some daft things at times – the likes of setting my hair alight in the bar at the Metropole in Birmingham at the Good Food Show. Fire alarms, fire engines, hotel evacuation, enough said. I didn't do that show again.

Throughout the journey the restaurant has always been a family affair. Rodney, my father, retired from his business to look after the wine side of the operation while Jean, my mother, who was one of the first to teach cookery to boys, looks after the restaurants' accounts and administration.

Then there's the team of chefs who have worked for me. One young lad who is now our head chef, Carl Tait, really did

We're famous Dad! Head chef Carl Tait with son, Louie

start at the bottom. He was 14 and had applied for a washing-up job. He showed great enthusiasm and very soon went from working a few nights a week to weekend work vegetable prepping, to the point of leaving school and coming in full-time as a commis chef. Ten years later he runs the kitchen when I'm not around. It's all about giving people a chance, just as I was given one.

I am so proud of what the team at Nutters has achieved – UK Restaurant of the Year, North-west Favourite Restaurant, a place in the AA's top 100 for its notable wine list and being named by The Times one of the top 10 celebrity chef restaurants in the UK.

Just like the food I prepare there, this book is created using good ingredients – experience, passion, and the refusal to accept second best.

And maybe just the odd dash of madness too. Because as you can probably see, I really am nuts.

But only about food.

NUTTER

NUTS!
ABOUT APPETISERS

BURY BLACK PUDDING AND DIVER-CAUGHT SCALLOPS WITH OLIVE OIL CRUSHED POTATOES

Simplicity is the key element in this recipe, with the true flavours of the ingredients being allowed to shine through.

INGREDIENTS (Serves 2)

For the olive oil mash

3 tablespoons olive oil

½ clove garlic, crushed

1 shallot, finely chopped

1 Desiree potato, peeled, cooked and flaked with a fork

1 tablespoon chives, chopped

2 tablespoons olive oil

1 horseshoe black pudding (R.S Irelands are regarded as the best)

6 plump fresh diver-caught scallops

To finish

Squeeze lemon juice

METHOD

1. For the olive oil mash, warm the olive oil and briefly fry the garlic and shallot until softened. Add the flaked Desiree potato and chives and mix well until all combined, season to taste and keep warm.

2. Slice the black pudding into 1cm discs, drizzle with 1 tablespoon olive oil and heat under a hot grill.

3. Heat the remaining oil in a frying pan and flash-sear the scallops until scorched on one side – turn and fry briefly on the other side taking care not to overcook them. Season.

4. Arrange the olive oil potatoes in the centre of a long plate – place alternate slices of the black pudding and scallops down the centre.

5. Serve immediately, finish with a squeeze of fresh lemon and share away...

BÖREK FRITTERS

T he local butchers hated me for serving this dish up on national TV. I had the Delia effect when everyone went out buying lamb mince. The flavours of this Middle Eastern appetiser work really well together. They are traditionally made with filo pastry, but I use spring roll pastry as it's crispier when deep fried. Alternatively, for a low-fat version, the finished parcels can be baked in a hot oven until crisp and golden.

INGREDIENTS *(Serves 4)*

1 tablespoon olive oil
1 onion, finely chopped
1 clove garlic, finely chopped
200g minced lamb
2 teapoons cumin
1 teaspoon ground coriander
100g feta cheese, diced
50g fresh spinach leaves, shredded
2 spring onions, chopped
Few sheets spring roll pastry

To serve
2 tablespoons olive oil
Few mixed salad leaves
100ml yoghurt
Squeeze fresh lemon

METHOD

1. Heat the olive oil. Fry the onion and garlic for 2-3 minutes until softened. Add the lamb, cumin and coriander and sauté for 5 minutes. Leave to cool.

2. Combine the cheese, spinach, spring onions and lamb mixture and season to taste.

3. Lay out the spring roll pastry. Place spoonfuls of the mixture at one end of the pastry, roll to form a triangle, then brush with water to help it stick.

4. Shallow fry in some hot vegetable oil for 2 minutes, until golden and crisp.

5. Serve the parcels with the yoghurt, lemon and salad leaves.

"
Rabbit. Rarebit. Rarbit.
There are endless arguments about what to
call it. Who cares? Just tuck in
"

NUTTER'S LANCASHIRE RAREBIT

Anthony Worrall Thompson says it's amazing, Michael Winner declared it the best he'd ever eaten. With praise like that, I can't keep it a secret any longer. Here it is, the ultimate in Welsh rarebit recipes.

There are many variations of this dish and endless hot air has been expended on debates about everything from the spelling of the name to whether you should put beer, wine or neither in the mix. But essentially the rarebit is a mixture of cheesy white sauce or grated cheese mixed with mustard and Worcestershire sauce.

In this recipe I use a crumbly Lancashire and stilton which gives it extra richness and a light blue colour. Other favourites are Red Leicester and a good Cheddar cheese.

INGREDIENTS (Serves 10)

400g Lancashire cheese, roughly chopped
200g stilton, roughly chopped
2fl oz milk
50g plain flour
50g breadcrumbs
1 egg
2 egg yolks
1 tablespoon Dijon mustard
2 tablespoons Worcestershire sauce
1 thin baguette, cut into rounds and lightly toasted

To serve
Few mixed salad leaves
Worcestershire sauce

METHOD

1. Place the Lancashire, stilton and milk into a casserole pan and heat slowly until the cheese melts.
2. Add the flour and breadcrumbs and cook out for 1 minute until the cheese thickens and comes away from the edge of the pan.
3. Remove from the heat, cool slightly then place in a food processor. Add the egg yolks, mustard and Worcestershire sauce and blend until smooth.
4. Take the slices of baguette, smear with the Welsh rarebit, glaze under a grill until lightly golden brown then serve with the salad leaves and Worcestershire sauce.
5. Any remaining rarebit can be kept in the fridge for up to a week.

CRISPY BURY BLACK PUDDING WONTONS

A Nutter classic and one that's become a bit of an institution here at the restaurant, selling over 75,000 portions since its appearance on the menu 16 years ago. The combination of the famous Bury black pudding with the Chinese influence of ginger and spring onions is totally awesome, even though I do say so myself.

This dish has gone through a bit of a makeover recently thanks to a food critic who said they looked like Spock's ears but tasted amazing. Beam me up Scotty.

INGREDIENTS *(Makes 50 wontons)*

1 tablespoon olive oil
1 small onion, finely chopped
1 clove garlic, finely chopped
2.5cm piece fresh ginger root, finely chopped
450g black pudding, skinned and chopped
8 spring onions, trimmed and finely chopped
140g boneless, skinless chicken breast, roughly chopped
25g butter, at room temperature
2 eggs
150ml whipping cream
Good pinch of freshly grated nutmeg
A few basil leaves, chopped
350g wonton skins
Vegetable oil, for deep-frying
Salt and fresh ground black pepper

METHOD

1. Heat the olive oil in a non-stick frying pan over medium heat. Gently fry the onion, garlic and ginger until soft. When they have softened, add the black pudding and cook for about 1 minute.

2. Add the spring onions then remove the pan from the heat so that they remain crunchy. Put it to one side to cool.

3. Blend the chicken breast in a food processor with 1 teaspoon of salt. Add the butter and blend again.

4. Now add 1 egg and continue to blend while you pour in the cream. Stop the motor from time to time and scrape the inside of the bowl with a rubber spatula so that everything is evenly combined.

5. Stir the chicken mousse into the black pudding mixture and season with salt, pepper and nutmeg. Finally, add the basil.

6. Lay out some of the wonton skins on a clean work surface and place a spoonful of the black pudding mixture in the centre of each.

7. Beat the remaining egg and use it to brush the edges of the wonton skins. Fold over to form a little parcel. Repeat until all the mixture has been used.

8. Deep fry in hot oil 180°c for about 2-3 minutes. Cook them in batches keeping them warm while you cook the rest.

Selling over 75,000 portions
these must be good!!

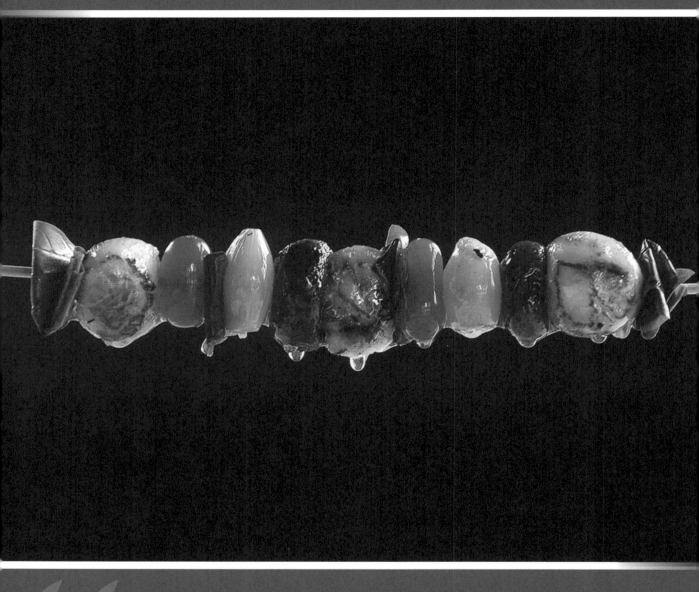

So ditch the blackened burger and savagely-burned sausage and try this designer kebab instead

BBQ QUEENIE SCALLOP KEBAB WITH GARLIC AND ROSEMARY OIL

You've seen the weather forecast for dazzling sunshine. So out comes the barbeque, which is an immediate cue for it to pee down with rain. Fear not. This recipe works equally well over the hot BBQ coals or under a hot grill indoors. Make sure you don't overcook as the scallops go rubbery.

INGREDIENTS *(Makes 10 kebabs)*

10 bamboo kebab skewers
20 baby onions peeled and blanched in hot water for 5 minutes
1 bunch fresh basil
20 small chestnut mushrooms
20 small vine tomatoes cut in half
30 queenie scallops - fresh rather than those frozen ones pumped with brine
4 tablespoons olive oil
1 sprig rosemary
1 clove garlic
Juice of ½ lemon

METHOD

1. First soak the skewers in water for about 10 minutes - this prevents them from burning on the BBQ.

2. Take each item and place alternate pieces on each stick - for the basil just bend each leaf into quarters and spike with the skewer.

3. In a mini liquidiser blend together the rosemary, garlic and lemon and drizzle over each kebab - season heavily then place over the hot charcoals.

4. Leave for 2 minutes then turn and cook for a further 2 minutes. Do not overcook them otherwise the scallops will toughen and go chewy.

5. Serve straight away with some nice mixed leaves and a light mayonnaise.

LOTUS CRISP

Forget Walkers, Doritos and Twiglets – Lotus crisps are the next big thing in designer cocktail snacks. The lotus root is the stem of the water lily, and it's used widely in Chinese and Japanese cuisine.

The root is first peeled then sliced horizontally to reveal a design of flower-like holes. It can be eaten raw or cooked and added to salads and stir-fries. If you're not using it straight away, store in water with a squeeze of lemon to prevent it turning brown. Personally I like it my way – dusted with a shower of cornflour then deep-fried until crispy and dunked into a tangy plum sauce.

INGREDIENTS (Serves 10)

1 x lotus root – weighing about 600g in total (they are available from Chinese supermarkets and generally each root is divided into 3 sections)

1 tablespoon cornflour

Vegetable oil for frying – heated to 180°c

METHOD

1. Peel each root and wash well under cold water. Pat dry then slice, either with a knife or a mandolin, into 1mm thin slices.
2. Lightly dust with the cornflour.
3. Cook in batches in the hot oil until crisp and golden, removing each batch with a spider.
4. Place on absorbent paper to remove any excess fat.
5. Season with sea salt then serve straight away or store in an air tight container for 2-3 days.

Smoked haddock gives the
dish extra depth

SMOKED HADDOCK, LANCASHIRE CHEESE AND SPRING ONION FISHCAKE

A right thrifty recipe that could be made from scratch using fresh fish or equally any leftover cooked fish and potato from a previous meal. You could say it's the perfect credit crunch lunch. I use smoked haddock in mine which I feel gives the cake extra depth. Calling it a cake always makes me laugh as it gives me flash backs to Peter Kay's Garlic Bread/Cheesecake sketch. Fish cake anyone?

INGREDIENTS *(Serves 4)*

2 Maris Piper potatoes, peeled and boiled until soft
150g smoked haddock fillet
2 tablespoons cream
1 clove garlic, crushed
50g Lancashire cheese, crumbled
4 spring onions, chopped finely
25g plain flour
1 egg, lightly beaten
25g dried white breadcrumbs
Vegetable oil for frying

To serve
Mixed salad leaves
Diced tomato
Chopped shallots

METHOD

1. Mash the potato through a ricer so there are no lumps.
2. Place the haddock on a small baking tray and pour over the cream and garlic. Roast in a hot oven for 3-4 minutes until it starts to flake. Remove from oven and leave to cool. Once cool, flake all the fish.
3. Mix together the potato, flaked haddock, spring onions and cheese. Season to taste.
4. Form into 4 'cakes' and then roll in the flour, egg and then the breadcrumbs.
5. Deep fry in some hot oil 180°c for 2 minutes until a light golden then place in a hot oven 180°c for 6 minutes.
6. Serve hot with some mixed leaves and a tomato and shallot salad if desired.

CRISPY HAGGIS FRITTERS WITH A NEEPS AND TATTIE SALAD

'll do anything to sell a few books to the Scots! – although they'll probably hurl me off the ramparts of Edinburgh Castle for tweaking their national dish. Joking aside, it's pretty damn tasty and the Lanark dressing just brings the dish together.

INGREDIENTS *(Serves 4)*

200g Haggis, lining removed and cut into cubes
55g flour
1 egg, lightly beaten
100g breadcrumbs
Vegetable oil for deep frying

For the dressing
1 egg yolk
1 tablespoon white wine vinegar
1 teaspoon Dijon mustard
100ml olive oil
25g Lanark blue cheese, crumbled

For the neep and tatties
1 small swede, cut into chunks, then boiled until soft
1 potato, cut into chunks, then boiled until soft
1 tablespoon white wine vinegar
3 tablespoons olive oil
Few strands of fresh tarragon

To serve
1 head red chicory
1 head white chicory
Few leaves of bulls blood
Bunch mizuna leaves

METHOD

1. Take the Haggis and toss in the flour, the egg and then the breadcrumbs, place in the fridge until ready to use.

2. For the dressing, blend the egg yolk, vinegar and mustard. Drizzle in the oil and mix in the cheese.

3. Combine the swede and potato, mash slightly then add the vinegar, oil and tarragon. Season to taste.

4. Heat the vegetable oil to 180°c and deep fry the Haggis until golden – drain.

5. Arrange the chicory, bulls blood and mizuna on a plate, place the neeps and tatties in the middle, arrange Haggis and finally drizzle over the dressing.

Perfect as a vegetarian starter

ROAST FIG TART WITH MAPLE AND SHERRY VINAIGRETTE

Perfect as a vegetarian starter – just make sure the figs are tender and ripe. Serve with mixed leaves and you could even throw in some crispy croutons for an extra crunch in your salad.

INGREDIENTS *(Serves 4)*

For the pastry
200g plain flour
100g butter, cubed and chilled
Pinch curry powder
Pinch poppy seeds
Water

For the filling
2 tablespoons olive oil
6 shallots, finely chopped
1 clove garlic
1 tablespoon honey
Few leaves fresh basil, shredded
150g goats cheese
4 ripe figs
4 teaspoons maple syrup

For the sherry vinaigrette
2 tablespoons sherry vinegar
6 tablespoons extra virgin olive oil
1 pinch sugar
Salt and pepper

To serve
Mixed baby leaves
Roma tomatoes, sliced in half

METHOD

1. For the pastry tartlets, place the flour in a bowl and rub in the butter until it resembles breadcrumbs. Add the curry and poppy seeds then enough water for it to come together to a firm dough. Leave to rest in the fridge for 10 minutes.

2. Dust a work surface with some plain flour then roll the pastry out thinly then divide between 4 individual tart cases. Prick with a fork then blind bake for 8 minutes until golden and crisp.

3. For the filling, heat the olive oil in a small pan and fry the shallots and garlic together for 5 minutes until softened. Add the honey and cook for a further minute. Leave to cool then add the basil and season.

4. Divide the shallot mixture between the 4 tartlet cases, crumble over the goats cheese. Slice the fig thinly and arrange on top. Finally drizzle over the maple syrup and season.

5. Bake in a hot oven (180°c) for 6 minutes to warm through.

6. Arrange the mixed leaves and tomatoes together on individual plates. Mix together the sherry vinaigrette ingredients and drizzle over the leaves before placing the tart on top.

SALT BEEF SALAD

It's a Nutter classic this one. It's my dad Rodney's recipe that was made regularly in his butchers shop in Prestwich. It's one of those old-fashioned English-style dishes perfect as a lunch dish, or served hot on freshly baked bread with a generous spoon of pickled shallots. Once cooked, the beef can be kept for over a week, because of the high salt content in the marinade. So it's great to have ready in the fridge for a lunchtime snack attack.

INGREDIENTS

For the marinade
900g table salt
200g salt petre
2000ml water
4 bay leaves
20 peppercorns
1.5kg silverside or beef brisket

For the cooking liquor
4 cloves garlic
Sprig fresh thyme
Sprig fresh rosemary
2 bay leaves

To serve
Butternut squash, roasted and freshly diced
Baby shoot salad
Parmesan wafer
1 tablespoon extra virgin olive oil

METHOD

1. Place the salt, salt petre, water, bay leaves and peppercorns into a pan, dissolve and bring to the boil, remove from heat and then leave to cool.

2. Add the silverside, cover with food wrap and leave in the fridge for one week.

3. Remove from the brine and wash under cold running water. Then place in a pan, cover with water, add the garlic, thyme, rosemary and bay leaves, bring to the boil and simmer for 2½ hours. Remove from heat, leave to cool in the liquor then place in the fridge overnight.

4. When ready to serve, remove from the cooking liquids, slice thinly and arrange on a plate with the butternut squash, baby shoots, parmesan and a drizzle of olive oil.

"Time is the vital ingredient.
But it's a dish worth waiting for"

"If you can't get hold of St George, try something like Perlwen, a Welsh Brie, or even a Cheshire Brie made with milk from Guernsey cows.

ST GEORGE'S FRITTERS

This was created for one of our St George's Day celebrations. And before you say it, no, the recipe doesn't call for dragon. It can be served as a starter or used as a canapé at a cocktail party. The cheese I use, oddly enough, is called St George. It's a camembert-style cheese made using goats milk from Nut Knowle Farm, World's End in East Sussex - It's really rich, creamy and dense.

INGREDIENTS *(Makes 20 Canapés)*

400g St George cheese, rind on
1 clove garlic, crushed
20 thin slices pickled ginger
50g flour
2 eggs, lightly beaten to mix
100g breadcrumbs
Vegetable oil for frying

To serve
Frisée salad, picked
Delicate plum sauce or tangy chutney

METHOD

1. Take the St George cheese and slice into even chunks, place in a bowl, add the garlic and toss gently.
2. Take a piece of the pickled ginger and stick into each chunk of cheese.
3. Toss the cheese pieces in the flour, shaking off any excess flour, roll in the egg and then in the breadcrumbs.
4. To get a crispier crunch - roll again in the egg and finally one last roll in the breadcrumbs.
5. Place in the fridge until ready to serve.
6. Heat the vegetable oil to 170°c and fry the fritters for 2-3 minutes until crisp and golden brown. Serve immediately - on their own or with your favourite dipping sauces or chutney.

(n)UTS! ABOUT SOUPS

Pumpkins come in many sizes, ranging from ½ kg to a colossal 450kg!

PUMPKIN AND CREAMY BUTTERNUT SQUASH SOUP

Oh boy, oh boy. This soup is truly one of the best ever. Smooth, velvety heaven. Ideal just after Halloween when all the shops want to clear their stock of pumpkins and you can get them at a bargain price.

Pumpkins come in many sizes, ranging from ½kg to a colossal 450kg! They are very versatile in cooking – there is a use for everything from the fleshy shell to the seeds and even to the flowers.

When ripe, the pumpkin can be boiled, steamed or roasted. It's great in pies, purée and soups.

INGREDIENTS *(Serves 4)*

600g pumpkin, peeled and chopped

600g butternut squash, peeled, deseeded and chopped

2 tablespoons olive oil

Pinch curry powder

2 tablespoons olive oil

1 small onion, chopped

1 clove garlic, chopped

1 small knob fresh root ginger, chopped

Pinch dried chilli flakes

1200ml chicken stock

200ml tin of coconut milk

Chopped coriander

METHOD

1. Prepare the pumpkin and butternut squash. Put in a roasting tin and sprinkle with olive oil and curry powder, then roast at 180°c for 15 minutes, stirring occasionally.

2. Heat the olive oil and fry the onion and garlic until softened.

3. Add the chicken stock and bring to the boil. Stir in the pumpkin, butternut squash, ginger and chilli and simmer for about 10 minutes until cooked through. Liquidise until smooth, pass through a sieve and season.

4. When ready to serve, reheat the soup, add the coconut milk to taste, adjust the seasoning, pour into a bowl and sprinkle with coriander if desired.

CREAMY CAULIFLOWER CHEESE SOUP

You'll find out later on in the book about my love of cauliflower cheese. Here it is in the form of a soup. Weird-sounding but amazing to eat, I serve it with black olive croutes which add an interesting crispness to the finished dish.

INGREDIENTS _(Serves 4)_

For the soup
25g butter
1 medium onion, peeled and coarsely chopped
1 clove garlic, peeled and chopped
1 stick of celery, coarsely chopped
1 pinch curry powder
225g cauliflower florets
300ml vegetable stock
300ml milk
60g creamy Lancashire cheese, grated

For the croutes
3 slices white bread
2 tablespoons olive oil
½ clove garlic, peeled and finely chopped
1 jar tapenade

METHOD

1. In a large saucepan, melt the butter and sauté the onion, garlic and celery for about 5 minutes over a low heat until they have softened but not coloured. Add the curry powder and cook for another minute.

2. Put in the cauliflower florets, the vegetable stock and the milk. Bring it to a simmer then cover the pan and cook until the cauliflower is tender, about 10 minutes. Remove it from the heat and leave it to cool before blending.

3. Cut the bread with a cutter into small rounds and place them on a baking sheet. Mix together the olive oil and garlic and drizzle over the bread. Spread the tapenade thinly over the top. Put the baking sheet in a hot oven (180°c) for about 5 minutes until the croutes are crispy.

4. Pour the soup into a liquidiser and blend until it is smooth. Rinse the pan and pour the soup back into it through a sieve, then return the pan to the heat.

5. Add the Lancashire cheese and continue to heat, stirring until the cheese has melted. Try not to boil the soup or the cheese will go a bit stringy. Taste and season, then serve it piping hot with the tapenade croutes on top or on the side.

"

Onion soup is one of the basics
of French cuisine

"

FRENCH ONION SOUP

It was a crisp January morning, the restaurant was closed for a few days after the New Year rush and I was enjoying a few leisurely days away with friends in New York. We'd just visited the site of the twin towers and, feeling a bit jaded, were looking for a decent place to eat to cheer ourselves up. We traipsed past many a diner but I wanted something better. I didn't know exactly what I wanted but a greasy hamburger with fries was not it.

I looked to the heavens for inspiration. It was then the sun broke through the clouds and shone a beam of sunlight upon the street beyond me. And there it was, Les Halles. Hallelujah!!! My prayers had been answered. It was a restaurant I'd always wanted to visit after reading about Anthony Bourdain's exploits in his book Kitchen Confidential. Even before we were through the door I knew what a great lunch was about to be had.

As expected, it wasn't formal, pricey, or over-fancy but just good, wholesome food with the execution nailed to perfection. We had the classic Gallic trio of French onion soup, duck confit, and crème brulée. I was in heaven.

The onions are cooked until tender and then caramelised to give the soup its characteristic intense colour and rich flavour. The soup is served in deep bowls with croutes, topped with grated cheese and then gratinated.

At Les Halles they line the empty bowl with croutes; sprinkle with cheese and then ladle the hot soup over the top. The croutes rise to the surface and are then browned under the grill and finally splashed with port.

INGREDIENTS (Serves 4)

75g butter
700g large onions, thinly sliced
1 clove garlic, crushed
2 teaspoon sugar
2 tablespoon plain flour
300ml port
300ml red wine
1500ml beef stock
Sprig rosemary, chopped

To finish
Toasted croutes
50g parmesan cheese, grated finely
50g cheddar cheese, grated finely
Splash port
Chopped chives

METHOD

1. Heat the butter and add the sliced onions. Toss in the butter then leave to fry for 5 minutes. Add the garlic and sugar and turn down the heat. Leave for about 20 minutes until the onions are stewed down and caramelised. Add the flour and stir in.

2. Deglaze the pan with the port and red wine and reduce by half. Add the beef stock and bring to the boil. Sprinkle in the rosemary and simmer very slowly for one hour. Season to taste.

3. Ladle between four deep bowls, top with the toasted croutes and scatter with the grated cheeses. Place under the grill to melt.

4. Finish with a drizzle of port and a sprinkling of chopped chives.

OXTAIL SOUP

T he phone rang from my photographer Tim Bradley. When he mentioned a Christmas photo shoot for my local newspaper and the fact he wanted to do the pictures in the snow, visions of a trip to Lapland were conjured up. Perhaps Switzerland?... or maybe even the North Pole? No, as it turned out. All the flights were full, so instead we ended up doing the photos at the Chill Factor at Trafford Park.

For when the real stuff starts to fall, homemade oxtail soup is one of the finest dishes around. It's rich, intense in flavour and full of goodness. Just make sure it's braised long enough so the meat flakes off the bone.

INGREDIENTS   (Serves 4)

1 oxtail, about 1.5kg – cut into 2cm chunks – ask your butcher to do it for you
2 tablespoons plain flour
2 tablespoons olive oil
2 rashers smoked bacon
2 cloves garlic, peeled
1 carrot, peeled and roughly chopped
1 stick celery, chopped
1 onion, chopped
400ml red wine
1500ml strong beef stock
Sprig fresh thyme
Sprig fresh rosemary

To finish
Crispy croutons
1 tablespoon olive oil
1 small carrot, peeled
1 small parsnip, peeled
Chopped chives
Flat leaf parsley

METHOD

1. Take the oxtail and dust with the plain flour. Heat the olive oil in a casserole pan, add the oxtail and brown on both sides.

2. Add the bacon, garlic, carrot, celery and onion and fry briefly. Add the red wine, beef stock, thyme and rosemary and bring to the boil – reduce the heat and simmer for 3 hours.

3. Remove the oxtail. Leave to cool slightly, then pick off the meat and place to one side.

4. Skim off any fat from the cooling liquor, reduce slightly and then pass through a sieve. Season to taste.

5. Take the carrot and parsnip and cut into a neat dice. Heat the olive oil and fry the vegetables until cooked through. Add the oxtail chunks and the chopped herbs.

6. Reheat the soup. Place the root vegetables and oxtail mix in a bowl, pour on the hot soup and serve with some crispy croutons.

"This soup, once made, can be chilled and then frozen ready to be reheated whenever you need your cockles warming!"

A taste sensation with

mini–explosions of sweet flavour

PEA AND POTATO SOUP WITH HAM HOCK CROSTINI

This fabulous soup is based on a classic leek and potato formula. It can be eaten hot or cold. The secret to this is using frozen petit pois puréed into the soup first and then finishing it off with fresh peas left whole at the end. The whole peas burst in your mouth, creating mini-explosions of sweetness after each mouthful.

INGREDIENTS *(Serves 4)*

450g ham hock, soaked in water overnight
2 bay leaves
1 clove garlic, chopped
1 carrot, onion and celery stick, each cut into small dice
2000ml chicken stock
2 Maris Piper potatoes, peeled and diced
400g frozen peas, defrosted

To serve
200g fresh peas, podded and blanched briefly
Crostini
Crème fraîche

METHOD

1. Place the ham hock in a casserole pan and add the bay leaf, garlic, onion, carrot, celery and chicken stock. Bring to the boil and simmer for 2 hours until the meat starts to fall off the bone.

2. Drain the meat and vegetables and reserve the stock.

3. Skim the stock to remove any scum and place back in the casserole pan, add the potatoes and cook until tender.

4. Add the peas and blend in a food processor until smooth. Pass through a sieve and season to taste.

5. Remove the meat from the bone and flake into pieces. Serve on the crostini with some of the vegetable mix.

6. Place some of the ham mixture into the bottom of each soup bowl, add some of the fresh peas and pour on the hot soup. Drizzle with the crème fraîche and serve.

PARSNIP AND TOMATO SOUP

H ere's a great autumnal soup. It's just perfect when the new season parsnips are coming through. Double up the recipe if you fancy and freeze half of it ready to pull out and heat for those times when you want a meal in a hurry.

INGREDIENTS

1 tablespoon olive oil
1 onion, chopped
2 cloves garlic, chopped
1 tablespoon tomato purée
1200ml vegetable stock
400g tinned plum tomatoes
600g parsnips, peeled and chopped
Sprig fresh rosemary

To finish
Crème fraîche
Basil oil - make by blending approx 20 basil leaves with 100ml olive oil
Hot crusty bread

METHOD

1. Heat the olive oil in a casserole pan. Fry the onion and garlic together until softened.
2. Add the tomato purée and cook out for a minute.
3. Add the vegetable stock and plum tomatoes and bring to the boil.
4. Add the parsnips and rosemary and simmer gently for 30 minutes or until the parsnips are cooked.
5. Blend in a liquidiser until smooth then pass through a sieve.
6. Season to taste. Serve piping hot with a drizzle of basil oil and a generous swirl of crème fraîche.

A soup to savour at its best
in late summer

VINE TOMATO AND SWEET POTATO SOUP WITH GARDEN HERB PESTO

This is the bee's knees at any time of year, but at its best in the late summer when our English tomatoes are falling off the vine. Out of season you could use tinned plum tomatoes instead. The addition of sweet potato thickens the soup and gives it an amazing velvety finish. The sweet potato, incidentally, is not a potato at all – it's the tuberous root of a tropical vine grown widely in South Africa.

INGREDIENTS *(Serves 4)*

2 tablespoons olive oil
2 cloves garlic, peeled
2 large onions, chopped
200ml red wine
1 tablespoon tomato purée
2 sweet potatoes, peeled and diced
900g vine tomatoes
850ml chicken stock
Sprigs of thyme
Sprigs of rosemary
2 tablespoons whipping cream

For the garden herb pesto
1 tablespoon toasted pine nuts
2 cloves garlic
150g grated parmesan cheese
2 tablespoons mixed soft herbs (basil, chives and parsley)
2 tablespoons olive oil

To serve
Toasted baguette bread
Crème fraîche

METHOD

1. In a large saucepan, heat the olive oil. Add the garlic and onions and sauté briefly. Add the red wine and reduce by half, then stir in the tomato purée, sweet potatoes and tomatoes.

2. Add the chicken stock, thyme and rosemary, bring to the boil and simmer for about 30 minutes.

3. Blend in a liquidiser, pass through a sieve, add the cream and season to taste.

4. For the pesto; blend together the toasted pine nuts, garlic, herbs, parmesan cheese and olive oil to a paste, season then refrigerate until needed.

5. When ready to serve, reheat the soup. Pour into bowls and drizzle with crème fraîche, smear the pesto onto the toasted bread and serve.

TURNIP SOUP WITH CHIVE AND BACON DUST

Eating out in restaurants can sometimes be a problem for chefs as they know how things should be served. This was brought home to me in a respected restaurant in Berlin. I ordered one of the house specials, turnip soup. Now you don't have to be Gordon Ramsay to know that when a bowl of lukewarm wallpaper paste is served to you, it isn't right, no matter which country you happen to be in. This was duly sent back to the kitchen. Ten minutes later another bowl is sent out. This time a liquid resembling dishwater arrived. I wasn't impressed, back to the kitchen again. I then encountered another problem. In this particular restaurant the kitchen closes at 9pm no matter what part of the meal you're up to. I looked at my watch. 9pm. I left famished. Top tip on eating out in Berlin. Avoid the soup. Either that, or order three hours in advance. Here's how it should be done.

INGREDIENTS *(Serves 4)*

1 tablespoon olive oil
4 rashers of streaky bacon, roughly chopped
1 onion, chopped
2 cloves of garlic
1 stick of celery, roughly chopped
1600ml chicken stock
200ml milk
1 small celeriac, peeled and roughly chopped
1000g of turnip, peeled and diced

To finish
Chopped chives
2 rashers of back bacon, baked until crisp.

METHOD

1. Heat the olive oil in a casserole pan. Fry the bacon until lightly coloured, add the onion, garlic and celery and sweat off for 5 minutes until softened.

2. Add the chicken stock and milk and bring to the boil, then stir in the celeriac and turnip and simmer for 20 minutes or until the vegetables are cooked.

3. Blend in a food processor until smooth and then pass through a sieve. Season to taste.

4. To finish; in a pestle and mortar, grind the bacon to a powder then add the chopped chives.

5. Pour the soup into serving bowls and then scatter over the bacon and chive dust.

6. Serve with some crusty bread or crispy croutons.

CREAMY JERUSALEM ARTICHOKE AND CELERIAC SOUP WITH CHORIZO WAFERS

A truly decadent winter soup that's sure to wow your friends. Just make sure you use a decent chicken stock as it gives the soup extra depth. Use the truffle oil as an optional extra. It is quite expensive but a little goes a long way and it really lifts the soup to the next level.

INGREDIENTS *(Serves 4)*

1 tablespoon olive oil
1 small onion, chopped
1 clove garlic, chopped
1000ml chicken stock
500g Jerusalem artichokes, peeled and chopped
1 celeriac, peeled and chopped
2 tablespoons crème fraîche

To finish
Spring roll pastry
Chorizo slices
White truffle oil

METHOD

1. Heat the olive oil and fry the onion and garlic until softened.
2. Pour in the chicken stock and bring to the boil, then add the artichokes and celeriac and simmer for about 20 minutes until cooked through. Liquidise until smooth, pass through a sieve and season.
3. To make the chorizo wafers, bake some spring roll pastry strips until crisp, then use them to sandwich with chorizo rounds that have also been baked until crisp.
4. When ready to serve, reheat the soup, spoon on the crème fraîche, adjust the seasoning and pour into a bowl. Finish with a few drops of white truffle oil and those crispy chorizo wafers.

nUTS!
ABOUT FISH/SHELLFISH

Full of robust, earthy flavours

HAKE WITH CONFETTI OF VEGETABLES AND GIROLLE MUSHROOMS

Hake is one of those fish that can take on really robust and earthy flavours – and this recipe uses ingredients that deliver exactly that. The wild girolles are classed, alongside ceps, as the most flavoursome mushrooms around.

Wash them well to remove any soil and dirt, but do not soak them, otherwise they act like a sponge and absorb too much water. Once washed, pat them dry with a paper towel. Girolles have a firm, yellowish-white fruity flesh with a slight pepper taste. They are the perfect accompaniment to chicken or fish.

INGREDIENTS   *(Serves 4)*

1 tablespoon olive oil
4 x 180g fillets of hake, skin on but boned
1 small carrot, cut into very small dice
½ courgette, cut into very small dice
1 tablespoon chives, chopped
1 tablespoon tomato sauce
1 teaspoon sugar
2 teaspoons Worcestershire sauce
Few splashes of Tabasco sauce
1 tablespoon olive oil
Salt and freshly ground pepper
1 knob of butter
1 shallot, chopped finely
½ clove garlic, chopped finely
120g girolle mushrooms

To finish
Squeeze fresh lemon
Mixed leaves

METHOD

1. Heat the olive oil in a non-stick pan and seal the fish, skin side down until golden. Turn the fish and continue cooking until it oozes milky fluids.

2. Mix together the carrot, courgette, chives, tomato sauce, sugar, Worcestershire sauce, Tabasco sauce, olive oil and season with salt and pepper.

3. In a small frying pan, melt the knob of butter and sweat off the shallot and garlic until softened. Add the girolles and stir gently. Cook until the liquids have evaporated and the mushrooms are cooked through. Season.

4. When ready to serve, place the vegetable mixture in a ring on the plate and arrange the salad leaves. Place the fish on top and finish with the girolle mushrooms and a squeeze of fresh lemon.

CLASSIC FISH PIE

Comfort dining is still very much in vogue. And what better dish to sum up the style than this fantastic fish pie? You don't necessarily need to buy large fillets of fish. Ask your fishmonger for any trimmings or substitute another white fish like pollock or cod, but try and include a smoked variety as it adds an extra dimension to the taste.

INGREDIENTS *(Serves 6)*

- 1 tablespoon olive oil
- 1 onion, finely chopped
- 1 clove garlic, finely chopped
- 1 small leek, shredded
- 600ml milk
- 150g hake, filleted, skinned and boned
- 115g salmon, filleted, skinned and boned
- 115g smoked haddock, filleted, skinned and boned
- 115g butter
- 115g flour
- 1 tablespoon chopped parsley
- 400g cooked Maris Piper potatoes, mashed
- 2 tablespoons cream
- 2 egg yolks

METHOD

1. Heat the olive oil in a small casserole pan and fry the onion, garlic and leek for 3 minutes until softened.

2. Add the milk and bring to a gentle simmer. Add the fish and poach briefly until the fish starts to flake.

3. Carefully strain through a sieve, reserving the milk cooking liquor.

4. Divide the fish and vegetable mixture between 6 buttered ramekins.

5. In a small saucepan melt the butter, add the flour and cook out for 1 minute. Slowly add the reserved milk liquor, stirring as you add to prevent lumps. Add the chopped parsley and season to taste.

6. Divide the parsley sauce between the ramekins.

7. Mix together the mashed potato, cream and egg yolks – season then pipe on top of the fish mixture.

8. Bake in a hot oven 180°c for 10 minutes until golden and bubbling.

9. Serve with a mixed salad and some chunks of fresh bread.

"Smoked fish adds an
extra dimension"

This fish is one of the kings
of the ocean

PAN-FRIED JOHN DORY WITH JERUSALEM ARTICHOKE PURÉE

Whenever I see John Dory on any menu I have to order it. To me it rates alongside Turbot as one of the kings of the ocean. Cooked simply with just a hint of garlic and lemon you just can't beat it. Serve with the artichoke purée as a great starter fish course or increase the amount of fish and serve with additional potatoes and vegetables as a more substantial meal.

INGREDIENTS *(Serves 2)*

For the purée
25g butter
200g Jerusalem artichokes, peeled and roughly chopped
150ml milk plus additional if needed

For the fish
1 tablespoon olive oil
2 x 180g John Dory fillets, skin on but boned
Pinch chopped garlic
Squeeze fresh lemon

To finish - optional
Sautéed wild mushrooms
Baby potatoes
Sprigs fresh herbs

METHOD

1. Start by making the purée. Heat the butter in a casserole pan and add the artichokes. Toss in the butter and fry for 2-3 minutes. Add the milk, cover and place on a low light for 30 minutes until the vegetable is very soft.

2. Cool slightly, then place in a food blender and liquidise until smooth. Add the additional milk if needed to bring the purée to an airy, almost mousse-like consistency. Season to taste.

3. For the fish, heat the olive oil in a non-stick pan. Place the fish into the pan, skin side down and fry until sealed. Turn the fish over and continue cooking until cooked through. Add the garlic and lemon and spoon over the fish.

4. When ready to serve, place a generous spoonful of the hot purée on a plate. Top with the fish and serve with the optional potatoes, herbs and mushrooms scattered around.

OYSTERS WITH BABY SHALLOT AND SHERRY VINEGAR

O h how I look back and laugh. Oysters were one of my pet hates at The Savoy. I had only just started my apprenticeship at 16 years old and twice ended up at the hospital with an oyster knife injury. I hated the look of these evil creatures and had never dared to eat one and vowed I never would.

Then one afternoon I was held down by two sous chefs and an oyster was forced down my throat. It entered my mouth and my whole body shuddered, tears filled my eyes and then I suddenly stopped squealing. What a revelation, the taste was just so clean, so fresh. 'Give me more' I screamed. What an initiation to a great produce.

Oh, by the way, one of the sous chefs was Giorgio Locatelli. Thanks mate.

INGREDIENTS *(Serves 4)*

12 pacific oysters
10 baby shallots or 2 large shallots, peeled and chopped finely
½ lemon
Few dashes sherry vinegar
Black pepper
Sea salt
1 tablespoon chopped chives
Few dashes Tabasco (optional)

METHOD

1. Open the oysters with an oyster knife and brush off any grit that might be in the shell.

2. Arrange on a bed of crushed ice then shower with shallots, lemon, vinegar, pepper, salt and chives.

3. Serve as soon as you can. Heaven!!

"You either love them or hate them. Two chefs held me down to help me decide."

"Firm, tasty and perfect with
a simple salad"

ROAST HALIBUT WITH PARMESAN AND SUMMER SHOOT SALAD

Caught around the Scottish coast and waters of the North Pacific, the halibut is the largest of all flat fish with an average weight of around 11-13½ kg, but they can grow to as much as 272kg. When the halibut is born, the eyes are on both sides of its head so it has to swim like a salmon. After about 6 months one eye will migrate to the other side of its head, making it look more like a flounder. Halibut can be found at depths as shallow as a few metres to hundreds of metres deep

If bought really fresh, simply pan-sear and serve with just a squeeze of lemon and grinding of sea salt and pepper, or try this simple salad which exemplifies how tasty this fish can be.

INGREDIENTS *(Serves 4)*

1 tablespoon olive oil
1 clove garlic, crushed
4 x 200g halibut steaks, filleted, skinned and boned
1 punnet Roma vine tomatoes, halved
100g fresh garden peas, podded and blanched briefly
1 punnet baby herb shoots
Mixed salad leaves

To finish
50g parmesan cheese
1 tablespoon white wine vinegar
3 tablespoons extra virgin olive oil
1 teapoon caster sugar

METHOD

1. Mix together the olive oil and garlic and drizzle over the halibut steaks.
2. Heat a non-stick frying pan and seal the halibut on both sides until lightly coloured.
3. Remove from the pan and place in a hot oven 180°c and cook for 5 minutes or until cooked through.
4. Whilst cooking, start to arrange the Roma tomatoes, peas, shoots and leaves on plates.
5. Remove the fish from the oven. Finely grate some parmesan over the top, then mix the vinegar, oil and sugar together, season, drizzle over the salad and finally top with the halibut.

ROAST COD WITH ROCKET AND SHERRY VINAIGRETTE

The inspiration for this comes from a recent trip to Palma. This tapas-style dish was a sheer delight to eat and oozes all the flavours of the Mediterranean. Cod is generally found living in deep water and cold northern seas but is used heavily in the cuisine of Spain and Portugal. This flaky white fish is ideal drizzled with olive oil and roasted. Eaten with rocket, it is the perfect marriage, with the nutty, peppery flavours of the bitter salad leaf shining through.

For more of a tapas dish, place all the salad ingredients on one plate, flake the cod on top and drizzle the dressing over – either way you're sure to enjoy.

INGREDIENTS *(Serves 4)*

2 tablespoons olive oil
4 x 175g fillets of cod, skin on
Few sprigs of fresh thyme and rosemary

For the salad
100g fine beans, blanched
80g pitted black olives
1 banana shallot, finely sliced
1 bunch of rocket leaves
2 floz sherry vinegar
6 floz extra virgin olive oil

METHOD

1. Smear the cod with the olive oil and scatter with sea salt and pepper
2. Heat a small frying pan and seal the cod skin down until crisp.
3. Take a small roasting tray and scatter with the sprigs of thyme and rosemary. Place the cod skin side up on top and place in a hot oven (180°c) for 8 minutes or until cooked through.
4. Arrange the fine beans on individual serving plates. Place the rocket leaves in the centre and scatter with the black olives and shallots.
6. Place the cooked cod on top and finally mix the vinegar and oil together, season then drizzle all over the fish and leaves.

“A combination that shouldn't work,
but it does
”

ROAST SEABASS WITH AVOCADO GUACAMOLE

Granted, avocado guacamole with fish isn't one of those classic combinations. But hey it works - the zingy lime, tang of the chillies and richness of the avocado all marry together. Either eat as it is for a light lunch or serve with some mashed potato for a more substantial dinner.

INGREDIENTS *(Serves 4)*

2 tablespoons olive oil

4 x 180g seabass fillet, skin on but boned

For the guacamole
1 shallot, finely chopped
½ green chilli, deseeded and finely chopped
1 clove of garlic
1 tablespoon coriander, chopped
1 teaspoon of salt
2 avocados, ripe, skinned and de-stoned
Juice of one lime

For the caramelised onions
2 tablespoons of olive oil
20 small button onions
2 tablespoons of runny honey

To serve
Mashed potatoes
Light vinaigrette

METHOD

1. To make the guacamole, place the shallot, chilli, garlic, coriander and salt into a food processor and blend to a paste. Add the avocado and lime juice and blend until the avocado breaks down. Season to taste.

2. For the onions, heat the olive oil and gently fry the onions until slightly coloured. Add the honey then place in a hot oven 180°c for about 15 minutes until cooked through. Stir every 5 minutes for a good glaze. Season.

3. When ready to serve, heat the olive oil in a pan and fry the seabass skin side down until coloured and crisp. Turn and cook for a further minute or until the fish is cooked through.

4. Arrange the baby onions, mashed potatoes and guacamole on a plate. Top with the fish and finally a drizzle of vinaigrette.

NUTTER'S FISH AND CHIPS

Oh, to be British! Alongside roast beef, Yorkshire pudding and toad in the hole, fish and chips reigns supreme as the very essence of traditional British food. Get the freshest fish and you really can't go wrong. In my version of the classic batter I've brought on board an extra flavour from the days of the British Empire, curry. Don't worry it's just a pinch – this is a vindaloo-free zone.

INGREDIENTS (Serves 4)

4 large baking potatoes, peeled
Vegetable oil for deep frying
4 x 140g pieces of haddock, skinned, boned and seasoned
50g plain flour

For the batter
225g self raising flour
1 teaspoon bicarbonate of soda
200ml water
1 tablespoon white wine vinegar
200ml Boddingtons beer
1 tablespoon fresh ginger, peeled and finely chopped
Pinch curry powder

To finish
Sea salt flakes
Fresh lemon
Malt vinegar

METHOD

1. Cut the potatoes into chips and dry them thoroughly. Heat a deep pan of oil to 120°c and deep-fry the chips for about 6 minutes until they are soft but scarcely coloured. Drain and reserve them. Increase the oil temperature to 180°c.

2. To make the batter, sift the self-raising flour and bicarbonate of soda into a bowl. Mix together the water, vinegar, Boddingtons, ginger, curry powder and pour it into the flour. Use a balloon whisk to combine the mixture to a smooth batter.

3. Dust the haddock with the flour, coat it in the batter and lower the pieces into the oil. Fry the fish for 4-5 minutes until it is a deep golden brown. Drain it and keep it warm in a low oven.

4. Replace the chips in the fryer and cook until they are golden brown and crisp. Drain them thoroughly, then stack them on each plate.

5. Serve the fish along side the chips, a shower of salt and a squeeze of lemon... and don't forget the vinegar.

A delicacy, one of the most tender parts of the fish

SEARED MONKFISH CHEEKS WITH CUCUMBER SPAGHETTI

Cheeks? Fish have cheeks? – they most certainly do, and in my view they are one of the tastiest parts of the fish. They're also quite a delicacy, as it's quite a laborious task to remove them. But it's rewarding as they are one of the most tender parts of the whole fish.

Cheeks are taken from many varieties of fish, particularly cod and grouper which have plumper cheeks, but one of my favourites is monkfish. Ask your fishmonger to reserve some for you, but please do not even think about buying fish cheeks at the counter on a busy Friday or Saturday or you will know what it means to get "The Fish Eye"!

INGREDIENTS *(Serves 4)*

1 tablespoon olive oil
12 monkfish cheeks
1 clove garlic, crushed
Zest of ½ lemon
150ml white wine
1 red pepper and 1 cucumber – peeled and cut into thin strips

To finish
Chopped chives
Chopped dill

METHOD

1. Heat the olive oil in a non-stick frying pan. Season the monkfish cheeks and seal until lightly coloured on both sides.

2. Place in a small roasting tray. Add the garlic, lemon zest and white wine. Cover with aluminium foil and place in a hot oven (180°c) for 8 minutes.

3. Mix together the cucumber and pepper and form a small pile in the middle of 4 plates. Arrange around the monkfish cheeks, spoon over any of the cooking liquor then finish with a shower of chopped chives and dill.

SEARED SALMON FILLET WITH TOASTED CASHEW AND LEMON PESTO

Who says a pesto needs to be made with pine nuts? Probably the inhabitants of Genoa where the sauce originates... but I digress. We ran out of pine nuts one day so I substituted cashew instead, added a touch of lemon and the sauce was born. It's dense, smooth, rich and has a truly decadent taste. Having only ever eaten cashews lightly roasted and salted as bar snacks before, I thought I'd Google them and found out they are native to Brazil and are grown inside a fruit called the cashew apple. Each apple only produces one nut and when ripe it protrudes below the fruit. You learn something new every day!!

INGREDIENTS *(Serves 4)*

For the cashew and lemon pesto
150g cashew nuts
1 clove garlic
100g parmesan cheese, grated
2 tablespoons olive oil
Juice half lemon

For the salmon
1 tablespoon olive oil
2 x 200g salmon fillets, skinned and boned

To serve
Roasted baby vine tomatoes
Beef tomato
Mixed leaves
Lemon
Extra virgin olive oil

METHOD

1. Place the cashew nuts and garlic on a tray and roast in a hot oven at 180°c for 5 minutes until lightly coloured. Leave to cool.

2. In a food processor blend together the nuts, garlic, parmesan and olive oil until it forms a paste. Then season to taste.

3. When ready to serve, heat the olive oil in a non-stick pan and sear the salmon on both sides. Top with the pesto and place under a hot grill for about 2 minutes until the cheese has melted in the pesto.

4. Arrange the tomatoes and baby salad leaves on a plate and season, place the salmon on top and finish with an extra squeeze of lemon and a drizzle of extra virgin olive oil.

> A magnificent marriage of
> the Welsh, the Roman
> and the Lancastrian

SEARED SALMON FILLET WITH NUTTER'S LANCASHIRE RAREBIT

One of my favourites. It eats like a dream, the sheer combination of salmon, tomatoes and a cheese topping takes you to heaven. In saying that put the Lancashire rarebit on top of anything and it tastes amazing.

INGREDIENTS (Serves 2)

For the tomatoes
10 baby Roma tomatoes
1 shallot, finely chopped
½ clove garlic
Few sprigs fresh thyme and rosemary
2 teaspoons balsamic vinegar
1 tablespoon olive oil

For the Welsh rarebit (see page 27)

For the salmon
2 x 180g salmon fillets, skinned and boned
Splash olive oil
Few strands fresh leek, blanched
Few leaves fresh basil

To finish
Basil oil
Few mixed leaves

METHOD

1. Slice the tomatoes in half and place on a tray cut side up. Shave off a touch of each one so they stand up. Mix together the shallot, garlic, thyme, rosemary, vinegar and olive oil and drizzle over the top. Place in a hot oven (180°c) for 8 minutes until blistered.

2. Slice the fillet salmon thinly and roll to form a pinwheel shape. Hold in place by tying it with a strand of the blanched leek.

3. Season the salmon and then seal on both sides until just cooked.

4. Place a leaf of basil on top of each fillet. Take the Welsh rarebit and cover the top of the salmon with it. Don't worry if you have any mixture over – it will keep in the fridge for up to a week.

5. Place under a hot grill until golden (approximately 2 minutes).

6. When ready to serve – arrange the Roma tomatoes and salad on a plate, top with the salmon and an additional splash of Worcester sauce if desired.

SQUID TEMPURA

Squid tempura is one of those classic Mediterranean snack foods eaten accompanied by the quirky Padron Peppers (you know the ones – one in ten are ferociously hot. You take a gamble when you eat them) a nice glass of chilled Chablis, and a suitable place for watching the world go by. For this recipe the body of the squid is cut into rounds but do watch the cooking time as when fried for too long the flesh toughens.

INGREDIENTS *(Serves 4)*

250g squid tubes, innards removed
1 pinch curry powder
2 teaspoons Worcestershire sauce

For the tempura batter
115g self-raising flour
Pinch bicarbonate soda
150ml water
Splash white wine vinegar
1 teaspoon dried chilli flakes
1 clove garlic chopped fine
1 knob fresh root ginger,
finely chopped
Plain flour
Vegetable oil for frying

To finish
Rocket leaves
Tartare sauce

METHOD

1. Take the squid tubes and cut into thin rings. Dust with the curry powder and add the Worcestershire sauce. Leave to marinade for about 10 minutes.

2. Mix together the self-raising flour, bicarbonate of soda and add just enough of the water to form a light batter. Add the vinegar, chilli flakes, garlic and ginger.

4. Season the squid then toss in the plain flour.

5. Place into the batter then fry in batches in the hot vegetable oil (180°c for 2-3 minutes) until crisp and a light golden colour.

6. Serve hot with the rocket and tartare sauce.

"To see a kitchen full of Italian mamas cooking all at the same time, was to see true passion for cooking"

SEARED SEABASS WITH CALDESI'S SAGE AND PUMPKIN GNOCCHI

Inspiration for dishes comes in many ways, whether it be from the seasonal fruit and vegetables in the markets or at my fishmonger for the daily catch. Other times it's a case of being inspired by others. I was invited to a function at the Caldesi De Campagne in Bray, Berkshire. Katie and Giancarlo Caldesi are friends of mine and happened to be promoting their new book 'Mama's Cookbook'. As a PR stunt they had invited all their chefs' mums across from Italy for a special gourmet evening where the mamas cooked their specialities. To see these ladies cook was sheer inspiration for me... and seeing them prepare my favourite Italian dish Gnocchi, I was in heaven. I even put it on my menu as Caldesi Style in honour of their passion for cooking.

INGREDIENTS   *(Serves 4)*

For the gnocchi
2 Maris Piper potatoes
1 egg
200g plain flour
4 fresh sage leaves, shredded
1 tablespoon olive oil
25g butter
50g semolina
1 small pumpkin or butternut squash, rind removed, flesh diced
2 tablespoons olive oil
Pinch curry powder
100g parmesan cheese
2 tablespoons balsamic vinegar
6 tablespoons olive oil
1 tablespoon olive oil
4 x 180g fillets seabass, skin on but boned

METHOD

1. Take the potatoes, skin on, and simmer in water until cooked, remove and whilst still warm peel and pass through a potato ricer.

2. Place in a bowl, mix in the egg, salt and pepper and sage. Flour a work surface and place the mixture in the centre. Gradually keep on mixing in flour until you get a smooth dough. Don't overwork otherwise it will become too heavy.

3. Roll the potato dough into cylinders and cut into pieces about 2cm wide. Then roll each piece over a fork to leave an indentation. Place on a tray with semolina until ready to cook.

4. Have a pan with boiling salted water ready. Place the gnocchi in the water and simmer until they rise to the surface. Remove with a slotted spoon, cool, then drizzle with olive oil to prevent sticking.

5. Place the pumpkin on a roasting tray, drizzle with olive oil and sprinkle with the curry powder. Roast in a hot oven, 180°c for approximately 15 minutes or until just cooked.

6. When ready to serve, heat the olive oil in a non-stick pan. Seal the seabass skin side down until crisp, turn over and carry on cooking until cooked through. Remove from the pan and keep warm.

7. When you're ready to serve, finish the gnocchi by first heating the remaining olive oil and butter. Sauté the gnocchi until hot and golden. Place on a plate, scatter on some parmesan shavings, the pumpkin chunks, the seabass and finally a drizzle of vinaigrette.

THAI-STYLE MUSSELS

I love mussels but only if they're really fresh, in season and nice and plump. I've given them an Asian style makeover which packs an awesome kick. Have some hot crusty bread ready at the end to mop up the juices.

If you're in a rush or your knife skills aren't so sharp, you could always blend up the onion, chilli, garlic, ginger, fennel and lemon grass in a food processor instead of chopping by hand.

INGREDIENTS *(Serves 2)*

2 tablespoons olive oil
1 small onion
1 red chilli, deseeded
1 clove garlic, 1 knob of fresh root ginger, ½ bulb fennel, ½ stalk lemon grass
1200g mussels
250ml dry white wine

To finish
50g coconut cream
1 tablespoon coriander roughly chopped
Squeeze fresh lime
2 spring onions, shredded

METHOD

1. Heat the olive oil in a large saucepan. Finely chop the onion, chilli, garlic, ginger, fennel and lemon grass and add to the pan. Sauté for 3-4 minutes until softened.

2. Add the mussels and white wine and cover. Cook over a high heat for approx 4 minutes, shaking the pan frequently until the mussels open.

3. Transfer the mussels to warmed serving bowls and add the coconut cream and coriander to the cooking liquor in the pan. Bring to the boil, season to taste, then pour over the mussels and serve immediately with a squeeze of fresh lime and a shower of spring onions.

" Be prepared – these are mussels
packing an awesome kick "

One for the special occasion

TURBOT WITH ENGLISH ASPARAGUS AND COURGETTE FRITTERS

Turbot is without doubt one of the kings of the ocean. It's firm white flesh has an amazing delicate flavour and is ideal for roasting, poaching or pan frying. It's quality does come at a premium price so save it for that special occasion.

INGREDIENTS *(Serves 4)*

1 large courgette
Pinch curry powder
50g plain flour
1 egg, lightly beaten
50g dry white breadcrumbs
Vegetable oil for deep frying
1 tablespoon olive oil
4 x 200g fillets of turbot, skinned and boned

For the dressing
2 tablespoons sherry vinegar
6 tablespoons extra virgin olive oil
Juice of ½ lemon

To finish
Vegetable balls
Mixed leaves
1 bunch English asparagus, trimmed and blanched

METHOD

1. Slice the courgette into ½ cm lozenges, season with salt and pepper and a pinch of curry powder.

2. Toss the courgettes in flour, then into the egg and finally into the breadcrumbs to get a nice even coating.

3. Deep fry in hot oil at 180°c for 2 minutes until a light golden colour. Keep warm.

4. Heat the olive oil in a non-stick pan, season the turbot then seal in the hot oil until lightly coloured. Turn and continue cooking until cooked through.

5. When ready to serve, arrange the salad, vegetable balls and asparagus on a plate. Add the warm courgette fritters, top with the turbot and finally mix the vinegar, oil and lemon together, add a good grinding of salt and pepper and drizzle over the top.

ROAST JOHN DORY WITH A WHITE ASPARAGUS AND GARDEN PEA DRESSING

D rawing inspiration from a recent trip to St. Tropez I thought I'd share with you this simple fish recipe that really brings the best out in the taste and texture of John Dory. Regarded as the king of the ocean, it's well worth sourcing out this fish. Just make sure it's really fresh and the vegetables under it are in season. If you can't get hold of white asparagus why not try the John Dory with the celeriac Remoulade on page 142 and serve with a rocket salad?

INGREDIENTS *(Serves 4)*

2 tablespoons olive oil

4 x 150g pieces of John Dory, skin on but boned

1 bunch white asparagus, peeled and blanched

50g fresh garden peas, podded and blanched

50g fresh broad beans, podded and blanched

1 small carrot, peeled, diced and blanched

For the dressing
2 tablespoons balsamic vinegar
6 tablespoons extra virgin olive oil

To finish
Few sprigs chervil and dill
½ lemon

METHOD

1. Heat the olive oil in a frying pan and seal the fish skin side down until lightly coloured. Turn over then place in an oven at 180°c for 4-5 minutes until cooked through.

2. Arrange the blanched vegetables on a plate (blanching simply means cooking them in a pan of boiling lightly salted water until al dente, then plunging into ice cold water to stop the cooking. This retains the colour, vitamins and minerals of the vegetable).

3. For the dressing; mix together the vinegar and oil and season to taste. Drizzle over the vegetables, place the cooked fish on top. Finish with a squeeze of lemon and finally a few sprigs of fresh herbs.

" Inspired by St. Tropez,
there can be little better "

Make a name for yourself with this dish. All you need is a summer day and some guests

ROAST COD WITH A GRIDDLED THAI RED ONION SALAD

This is impressive any time it's served up. But to really earn a name for yourself, do the griddling on the barbecue and dish it up to your guests outside on a summer day. It certainly makes a bigger impact than burger and sausage.

INGREDIENTS *(Serves 2)*

2 x 200g fillets of cod, skin on but boned
1 tablespoon olive oil
1 red onion, peeled and cut into wedges
6 new potatoes, cooked skin on, cooled and halved
1 clove garlic
Pinch fresh root ginger, finely chopped
½ red chilli, deseeded and finely chopped
4 spring onions, finely chopped
1 teaspoon caster sugar
1 tablespoon sherry vinegar
3 tablespoons extra virgin olive oil
To finish
Few leaves fresh coriander, chopped
½ lime, sliced into thin segments

METHOD

1. Heat the olive oil in a non-stick pan and seal the fish skin side down until lightly coloured. Seal the other side, then place on a baking tray and into a hot oven (180°c) for about 6 minutes until cooked through.

2. Drizzle the olive oil over the onions and potatoes and place in a hot griddle pan until lightly charred. Season to taste.

3. In a small pan, sweat off the garlic, ginger and chilli in a splash of olive oil for 2 minutes until softened. Remove from the heat and stir in the spring onions, sugar, vinegar and oil.

4. Arrange the potatoes and red onion on a plate. Scatter with the garlic and ginger dressing then place the cod on top and finish with the lime segments and coriander.

SLOW-BRAISED PORK BELLY WITH A HOT BEAN CASSEROLE

Cooking on a limited budget does not have to mean bland, boring food. Sometimes it just takes a bit of inspiration to utilise produce to its best potential. Take pork belly – so underused and you can pick it up cheaply. The secret to this dish is the very slow-braising of the pork.

Eat hot and leave the trimming. Slice thinly and it makes the most amazing pork sandwiches. Two meals in one!

INGREDIENTS *(Serves 4)*

1 tablespoon olive oil
2 cloves garlic, chopped
1 onion
1 tablespoon thyme and rosemary, chopped
1 x 2kg pork belly, rind removed and left flat
2 tablespoons olive oil
1 carrot, diced
1 stick celery, diced
1 onion, finely chopped
4 cloves garlic
1 cinnamon stick
1 small knob fresh root ginger, chopped
200ml soy sauce
2 litres beef stock
1 tablespoon tomato purée
Splash Worcestershire sauce
400g borlotti beans, soaked overnight

To finish
1 bunch spring onions, shredded
1 chilli, finely shredded

METHOD

1. Heat the olive oil and fry the garlic, onion and herbs for 3 minutes until softened.

2. Take the pork belly and top with the onion mixture – roll into a tight cylinder and tie with string.

3. Heat the olive oil and fry the pork belly until coloured on all sides. Add the carrot, celery, onion, ginger, garlic and cinnamon and fry briefly then stir in the soy sauce, beef stock, tomato purée and Worcestershire sauce. Cover with tin foil and place in a hot oven 140°c for 2½ hours.

4. Remove the pork from the pan and leave to cool, then roll tightly in tin foil. Skim off any fat from the cooking liquor. Add the beans and simmer for 1 hour until the beans are tender.

5. When ready to serve, carve the pork into 2cm thick slices. Fry in a pan until crisp or heat in the oven. Serve with the hot bean casserole, scattered with sautéed spring onions and chillies.

6. Any remaining meat can be refridgerated for up to a week – sliced thinly and fried until crisp, it makes the most amazing pork sandwiches. Two meals in one!!

Any leftovers make the most amazing pork sandwiches

"Hungry? This is a he-man of a breakfast to kick sand in the face of all the wimpy alternatives"

BEEF FILLET WITH DESIGNER BREAKFAST

A proper man's plate. Protein, protein, protein combining all the elements of an all-day breakfast but served up in true Nutter style.

INGREDIENTS *(Serves 2)*

1 tablespoon olive oil
2 Cumberland sausages
4 rashers streaky bacon
Few slices from a horseshoe black pudding
6 small new potatoes, blanched in simmering water
3 Roma tomatoes, halved
4 chestnut mushrooms, halved then sautéed in a touch of butter and seasoned
1 tablespoon olive oil
1 knob butter
2 x 175g beef fillet
1 clove garlic
2 tablespoons brandy
100ml red wine
100ml strong beef stock

To finish
1 tablespoon olive oil
2 quails eggs
Few sprigs flat leaf parsley

METHOD

1. Place the sausages and bacon on a small tray then drizzle with the olive oil. Roast in a hot oven (180°c) for 10 minutes until the sausage is cooked and the bacon crisp. Leave to cool then slice the sausage into lozenges.

2. Get a tray ready to go in the oven with the sliced sausages, bacon, black pudding, potatoes, tomatoes and mushrooms. This will be warmed through in the oven 5 minutes before you serve up.

3. For the steak; heat the olive oil, adding a knob of butter. When foaming add the steak and seal in the hot pan. Turn, then continue cooking until it is done to your liking. Remove from pan, keep warm then pour off any excess fat.

4. De-glaze the pan with the brandy and red wine, reduce by half then add the beef stock. Reduce again then finally add the cream and adjust the seasoning.

5. In a small non-stick pan, heat the olive oil then carefully break in the eggs. Cook until the white is set but the yolk is still runny.

6. Take your warmed through breakfast mixture, arrange on a serving plate and place the rested steak on top with a few spoonfuls of your red wine sauce and finally finish with the cooked quail egg and a few herb sprigs.

CLASSIC BRAISED LAMB SHANK WITH PORT REDUCTION

Now here's a really gutsy, hearty dish. The lamb shank cooks best using a method of cooking where there's plenty of moisture such as braising, stewing or very slow roasting done over a long period of time. This dish can be served straight away, or done the day before, refrigerated and reheated 20 minutes before serving. That makes it ideal for stress-free entertaining.

INGREDIENTS *(Serves 4)*

1 tablespoon olive oil
4 lamb shanks (about 450kg each)
1 carrot, diced
1 stick celery, diced
2 cloves garlic, chopped
1 onion, chopped
Sprigs thyme and rosemary
200ml port
200ml red wine
800ml beef stock

To serve
Crushed potatoes, onions, baby parsnips, carrots and herb sprigs

METHOD

1. Heat the olive oil in a casserole pan and brown the lamb shanks on all sides.

2. Add the carrot, celery, garlic and onion and soften, then the thyme, rosemary, port, red wine and beef stock.

3. Cover with tin foil and place in a hot oven (150°c) for about 2½ hours until tender. Check halfway through to ensure there is enough liquor for the lamb to braise in.

4. Remove from oven and leave to cool.

5. Pass off about 400ml of the cooking liquor, skim off any fat, place in a pan and reduce by half. This forms your finished lamb sauce.

6. When ready to serve, arrange the hot potatoes and vegetables on a plate, place the lamb on top and finish with the hot lamb sauce spooned over.

"Ordinary chicken legs will never seem the same again"

BBQ POUSSIN LEGS WITH CUMIN AND CORIANDER

Here's barbecue finger food par excellence. It's a great alternative to your normal chicken legs as it cooks quicker and the meat is a lot sweeter. If you can't get poussin legs serve 1 chicken leg per person and increase the cooking time.

INGREDIENTS *(Serves 4)*

20 poussin legs
2 cloves garlic, chopped
1 small knob fresh root ginger, chopped
1 teaspoon cumin
1 teaspoon ground coriander
Pinch curry powder
Pinch fennel seed
Pinch dried chilli flakes
100ml olive oil

METHOD

1. In a mixing bowl combine the garlic, ginger, cumin, coriander, curry, fennel seed, chilli flakes and olive oil and mix well.

2. Coat the poussin legs in the marinade with a good grinding of salt and pepper. Leave in the fridge for at least 1 hour.

3. When ready to cook, ensure your barbeque coals are nice and hot. Place the poussin legs around the edge of the grill, cooking for about 10 minutes until the bone pulls freely from the flesh.

4. Move the legs to the centre of the barbeque for a final finish which will crisp the skin.

5. Remove and serve. Finger licking good!!

SUPREME OF CHICKEN WITH CHRISTMAS DINNER FRITTER

Celebrate Christmas with a feast fit for a king. This is a great twist on your classic Christmas dinner and the best bit is it doesn't take hours to cook. All the tastes and flavours of a traditional Christmas dinner are combined in an amazing spring roll-style dish (spring roll pastry is available from most Chinese supermarkets, but if you can't get hold of it use a few sheets of filo instead).

As an additional side dish, shred up some more baby sprouts and sauté them for 2-3 minutes in a pan with some ginger, garlic, chillies and fresh coriander. It's a taste explosion!

INGREDIENTS *(Serves 4)*

4 x 170g supreme of corn-fed chicken, skin on
Few leaves of fresh Basil
Salt and freshly ground pepper
Dashes of olive oil

For the Christmas dinner fritters
1 tablespoon olive oil
2 rashers of smoked bacon, chopped
2 onions, finely chopped
1 chicken supreme, thinly diced
1 garlic clove, chopped
10 sprouts, finely shredded
1 cooked sausage, diced
2 spring onions, chopped
1 tablespoon chives, chopped
1 potato, cooked and mashed
4 sheets of spring roll pastry
1 egg, beaten
Vegetable oil, for deep-frying

For the sauce
1 tablespoon olive oil
2 shallots, finely chopped
2 tablespoons brandy
300ml port
600ml beef stock
Few fresh sage leaves
Salt and freshly ground pepper

METHOD

1. To make the Christmas dinner fritter; heat the olive oil in a frying pan and fry the bacon until golden. Add the onion, diced chicken and garlic and fry, stirring, until cooked through.

2. Stir in the sprouts, sausage, spring onion, chives and mashed potato and leave to cool. Season to taste.

3. Take the 4 chicken supreme, pull back the skin and press a few basil leaves onto the flesh of each one and cover with the skin again. Season with salt and freshly-ground pepper.

4. In an ovenproof frying pan, heat the olive oil. Add in the chicken supreme and sear on both sides. Place in a hot oven (180°c) for 6-8 minutes until cooked through.

5. Meanwhile, make the fritters. Lay out the spring roll pastry sheets and place a few tablespoons of the Christmas dinner fritter mixture running along the bottom edge.

6. Brush the pastry edges with the beaten egg and roll into a fritter shape, pressing firmly to seal the edges. Repeat the process, making 4 in all.

7. Heat vegetable oil (180°c) in a deep-fat fryer and deep-fry the fritters for 4 minutes until golden brown. Remove with a slotted spoon and drain on kitchen paper, then keep warm.

8. To make the sauce, heat the olive oil in a saucepan. Fry the shallots gently until softened.

9. Pour over the brandy and carefully flambé, burning off the alcohol. Add the port and reduce by half.

10. Add the stock and continue to reduce. Pass through a sieve and season to taste.

11. When ready to serve, place a fritter and a portion of chicken on each plate. Spoon around the sauce and serve with your choice of vegetables.

Bound to create an impression — since half your dinner guests will be wondering what kohlrabi is

SLOW-BRAISED LAMB SHOULDER WITH KOHLRABI CHUNKS

A real gutsy autumnal salad, using the last of the English tomatoes and the new season crop of kohlrabi coming through.

Kohlrabi, related to the turnip, is a fabulous versatile vegetable. It's great in purees but also is fantastic in salads and added to stews. It has a great fresh peppery taste.

INGREDIENTS *(Serves 4)*

1 tablespoon olive oil
1 onion, finely chopped
2 cloves garlic
1 tablespoon tomato purée
1 tablespoon chopped rosemary
2.5kg lamb shoulder, boned
2 handfuls of mirepoix (mixture of chopped celery, leeks, onion and carrot)
500ml red wine
1500ml beef stock

For the braised kohlrabi
2 kohlrabi
200ml chicken stock
25g melted butter

To serve
Griddled new potatoes
Tomato chutney, (see page 136)
Mixed leaves

METHOD

1. Heat the olive oil and sauté the onion and garlic together for 5 minutes. Add the tomato purée and rosemary and cook for a further 2 minutes. Leave to cool.

2. Take the lamb shoulder, season and smear the tomato mixture on the meat side. Roll tightly into a barrel and secure with string.

3. Heat a casserole pan, add a splash of olive oil and seal the lamb on all sides. Add the mirepoix, red wine and beef stock, cover with a lid and braise in a hot oven 140°c for 2½ hours.

4. Remove from oven, leave to cool then wrap tightly in food wrap and place in fridge.

5. Peel the kohlrabi to get rid of the tough outer skin. Cut into cubes roughly 1cm thick. Place in a small pan and cover with the chicken stock. Bring to the boil and add the butter. Simmer for about 15 minutes until cooked through.

6. Remove the kohlrabi with a slotted spoon and keep warm. Reduce the cooking liquor until only 1 tablespoon remains then return the kohlrabi back to the pan and toss in the reduction. Season to taste.

7. When ready to serve, slice the lamb into about 2cm thick slices, heat under a hot grill or fry in a pan until hot and golden.

8. Arrange the potatoes, kohlrabi and leaves on a plate. Place the hot lamb on top, a spoon of the tomato chutney and finish with a drizzle of balsamic vinaigrette.

CRISPY GOOSNARGH DUCK CONFIT

One of the great French classics that in its purest form is a preserve of the duck leg that every French housewife would have in her pantry. The French would generally warm the duck legs through with the bone still in and serve it as part of a cassoulet. I prefer to remove all the bones and crisp the skin under a hot grill which creates a crackling effect on top of the tender pieces of duck. Have a simple salad to go with it. 1-0 to England!

INGREDIENTS *(Serves 4)*

4 duck legs, preferably from Goosnargh
8 tablespoons salt
500ml goose fat
1 tablespoon olive oil
2 courgettes, sliced 1cm thick
100g parmesan cheese
Few mixed salad leaves
Drizzle of your favourite dressing

METHOD

1. Rub the duck legs with the salt and leave in the fridge overnight. Wash the salt off, place in a small deep baking dish and cover with the goose fat. Place in an oven 120°c for 2½ hours or until the meat comes cleanly away from the bone when pulled.

2. If serving straight away remove from the fat, remove the bones and place under a hot grill for about 2-3 minutes until crispy. Alternatively, if not serving immediately, leave to cool in the fat then place in the fridge, still covered in the fat and it will keep for a good week. Don't throw the fat away as it keeps for ages in the fridge and also gets more depth of flavour the more you use it.

3. Smear the courgette slices with the olive oil and chargrill them on one side, remove and season.

4. Arrange the courgettes on a plate, add some salad leaves, a few shavings of parmesan, a drizzle of your favourite dressing and finally top with that crispy duck.

It's a French classic, but England's winning ways make it extra special

"Roll it up in a tortilla to create an amazing midnight snack"

SEARED RUMP OF LAMB CHERMOULA

O f all the ways of cooking lamb this is the one I favour. The rump is seared in hot oil until the fat has caramelised, sprinkled with the Chermoula spices, cooked till pink then served sliced with a cool crème fraîche. It makes the most amazing midnight snack rolled up in a tortilla wrap.

Traditionally the meat is left to marinade in the Chermoula spices overnight and then fried but I find it overpowers the delicate flavours of the lamb. That's why I opt to sear it at the very last minute and toast the spices.

INGREDIENTS *(Serves 4)*

2 tablespoons of olive oil
4 x 160g rump of lamb
2 cloves garlic, crushed
2 teaspoons cayenne
2 teaspoons paprika
2 teaspoons cumin
Zest and juice of ½ lemon
2 tablespoons of coriander, chopped
1 tablespoon of flat leaf parsley, chopped
1 cucumber, cut into spaghetti strips
6 tablespoons crème fraîche
Juice ½ lemon
Few leaves fresh coriander

METHOD

1. Heat the olive oil. Season the rump of lamb and seal on both sides.

2. Mix together the garlic, cayenne, paprika, cumin, lemon, coriander and parsley. Scatter over the lamb then place in a hot oven (180ºc) for 5 minutes or until cooked to your liking. Leave to rest.

3. Mix together the crème fraîche, lemon and coriander. Season and place in the fridge until the lamb is ready.

4. When ready to serve, arrange the cucumber spaghetti on a plate, slice the loin of lamb and place on top and finally serve with the lemon crème fraîche.

SEARED VENISON FILLET WITH PINK PEPPERCORNS AND TOASTED SESAME

Venison is the meat of the moment. Sure, you may like it because you're heath-conscious and it's low in cholesterol. But it finds favour in the Nutter's kitchens because it's tasty and you can create some great dishes with it.

I buy mine from the Tatton Estate near Knutsford – the deer roam freely in the grounds eating a mixture of grass, hob nuts and wild herbs and are only killed to control the population.

The dark red and finely-grained meat of the deer is used in a number of ways. The haunch is usually roasted or it can be stewed or braised. But the best in my opinion is tenderloin from the saddle which can be cut into steaks and pan-fried, or done as in this recipe, which is reminiscent of a carpaccio of beef.

INGREDIENTS *(Serves 2)*

2 x 200g loins of venison, trimmed
1 tablespoon Dijon mustard
1 tablespoon pink peppercorns
1 tablespoon mustard seeds
1 tablespoon sesame seeds
1 tablespoon olive oil

To serve
Mixed salad leaves
Shizu cress (optional)
Few pink peppercorns
1 teaspoon toasted sesame oil
1 lime

METHOD

1. Take each loin of venison and smear with the Dijon mustard and a good grinding of salt and pepper.

2. Mix together the peppercorns, mustard seeds and sesame seeds and roll each venison fillet in the mixture – pressing the seeds against the venison so they stick.

3. Heat the olive oil in a frying pan until moderately hot and seal the venison fillet on all sides, turning as the seeds are toasted. Remove from the pan and leave to cool, then wrap in food wrap and refrigerate until ready to serve.

4. When ready to serve remove the venison from the food wrap and slice into thin slices. It should be charred on the outside but still very pink in the middle.

5. Arrange the venison on a plate with your favourite salad leaves tossed in vinaigrette. Finish with a scattering of pink peppercorns, a drizzle of toasted sesame oil and a squeeze of fresh lime.

An inspiration for jaded tastebuds

ROAST GUINEA FOWL WITH A DESIGNER HOT POT PIE

Tired of your bland, fried chicken breast? This will inspire those jaded tastebuds. Guinea fowl has a fabulous, earthy, robust taste which to me smacks of what chicken used to taste like years ago before all those artificial feeds came into use in the poultry industry. Cook it in the same way you would a chicken and just taste the difference.

INGREDIENTS (Serves 4)

2 whole guinea fowl (approx. 1kg each)
500ml chicken stock
200ml red wine
1 carrot and 1 stick celery, diced finely
1 onion, finely chopped
2 cloves garlic, chopped

For the pastry
200g plain flour
100g butter, chilled
Pinch curry powder
1 teaspoon poppy seeds
Water

For the cabbage
1 tablespoon olive oil
2 rashers bacon, cut into thin strips
1 shallot, finely chopped
1 clove garlic, finely chopped
½ small savoy cabbage, finely shredded
100ml white wine
200ml whipping cream

METHOD

1. Remove the breasts and legs from the guinea fowl. Place the legs in a casserole pan with the chicken stock, red wine, carrot, celery, onion and garlic and simmer gently for 1 hour. Take out the legs and leave to cool. Reduce the cooking liquor by half and leave to cool.

2. Remove the skin from the guinea fowl legs and flake the flesh into small pieces. Season and place in small ramekin dishes. Add some of the vegetables and the reduced red wine liquor.

3. For the pastry, rub the butter into the flour to form a breadcrumb consistency. Add the curry powder and poppy seeds and just enough water for the mix to come together to form a soft dough. Leave to firm in the fridge for 20 minutes.

4. Roll out onto a floured board and cut into rounds just slightly bigger than the ramekin. Brush the ramekin ridge with a touch of water, place the pastry on top and pinch. Leave in fridge until ready to use.

5. When ready to serve, bake at 180°c for 12 minutes until the pastry is cooked and golden.

6. Heat the olive oil in a sauté pan. Season the guinea fowl breasts then place in the pan skin side down. Cook until golden on both sides. Remove from the pan, then roast for 10 minutes(180°c) until cooked through.

7. Add the bacon to the pan you used to sear the guinea fowl and fry for 2 minutes. Stir in the onion and garlic and fry for a further 2 minutes then add the cabbage. De-glaze with the white wine and then stir in the cream. Season to taste.

8. Serve the hot pot pie with the creamy cabbage and guinea fowl breast.

SLOW-BRAISED SHOULDER OF LAMB WITH LOTUS CRISP

If you want a meat dish that simply melts in your mouth - this is the one for you. The key element is the slow braising, which keeps the meat oh so tender. If you don't use all the meat in one meal, it will keep in the fridge for a good few days.

INGREDIENTS *(Serves 4)*

1 tablespoon olive oil
4 shallots, finely chopped
2 cloves garlic, chopped
1 teaspoon rosemary, chopped
Few leaves fresh mint shredded
2.5kg lamb shoulder, boned
2 tablespoons olive oil
1 carrot and 2 sticks celery, roughly chopped
1 onion, roughly chopped
1 tablespoon tomato purée
Sprig of thyme and rosemary
300ml red wine
2000ml beef stock
25g butter

To finish
Sautéed sugar snap peas
Mashed potato
Balls of carrot/courgette
Lotus crisp (see page 32)

METHOD

1. Heat the olive oil and add the shallots, garlic and rosemary. Sauté briefly for 3-4 minutes, remove from the heat. Leave to cool then add the mint.
2. Take the lamb shoulder and season both sides. Lay the fat side down on a chopping board and scatter the shallot mixture on top.
3. Roll the shoulder into a cylinder and secure with string to hold it in place
4. Heat the olive oil in a casserole pan and seal the lamb until golden on all sides.
5. Add the carrot, celery and onion and sauté in the pan for about 2-3 minutes. Add the tomato purée, thyme, rosemary, red wine and beef stock. Bring to a gentle simmer, cover with foil and place in an oven at 140°c for 2½ hours.
6. Check the lamb is cooked properly; the meat should flake easily when cut with a knife. If not, return to the oven for a further 20 minutes.
7. Remove the lamb from the cooking liquor and roll tightly in tin foil (this keeps the lamb in a neat cylinder shape). Leave to cool then put in fridge until ready to serve. Strain the liquor through a sieve.
8. Unroll the lamb from the foil and remove the strings. Cut into 6 even slices. Heat the butter in a small frying pan and fry the lamb on both sides until golden. Place in oven at 180°c for 5 minutes to heat through.
9. Heat the cooking liquor and skim off any excess fat from the surface. Season to taste and reduce to thicken if necessary.
10. Place some of the sautéed sugar snaps in a bowl, place the lamb on top and finish with the mash, vegetable balls, lotus crisp and finally pour over the sauce.

Keep it nice and slow,
it's worth waiting for

"Well done, medium and rare all in one — a steak to please everyone"

SEARED BEEF FILLET WITH MIZUNA AND BACON BITS

You don't need a lot of beef to make this designer salad so seek out the best quality you can. Quite uniquely the meat is only seared on one side – resulting in a steak that is charred on the bottom, medium in the middle and rare on top. Beautiful. If you do want a more substantial salad just increase the quantity of meat and leaves.

Unsure about what mizuna is? It's a variety of rocket leaf which gives a peppery kick.

INGREDIENTS *(Serves 2)*

For the croutons
4 tablespoons olive oil
1 slice of white bread, placed in the freezer for 5 minutes (this eases slicing)
1 clove garlic, crushed
3 slices streaky bacon, cooked until crisp and cut into splinters

For the potato
2 tablespoons olive oil
1 small potato, peeled and finely diced
1 sprig fresh rosemary, chopped

For the beef
2 tablespoons olive oil
1 knob butter
2 x 85g slices of beef fillet

To serve
Mizuna salad
Mixed leaves
Simple vinaigrette

METHOD

1. Take the chilled piece of bread and cut into neat dice. Heat the olive oil and fry the bread, tossing frequently until a light golden colour. Add the garlic and toss a few more times.

2. For the potato, heat the olive oil in a non-stick pan and fry the potato cubes. Toss until the potato is cooked through and golden on the outside. Add the rosemary and toss a few more times. Season.

3. When ready to serve, heat the remaining oil in a pan and add the knob of butter. When it is foaming, add the steak and fry on a high heat until the blood starts to form on the top of the steak – only fry on one side.

4. Arrange the salad leaves on a plate, then scatter on the croutons, potato and bacon. Place the steak on top and finish with a drizzle of vinaigrette.

(n)UTS! ABOUT VEGETABLES & ACCOMPANIMENTS

CHICORY, ORANGE AND WATERCRESS SALAD WITH A PEA TOP AND NASTURTIUM FLOURISH

This salad was designed to showcase the produce growing on Aralia design's kitchen garden at the Chelsea Flower Show. It had an amazing edible wall where I was just able to pick what I wanted, throw it into a bowl and voila!

Bitter, sweet and peppery, the perfect accompaniment to a barbeque rib-eye steak, a seared fillet of fish or even scatter with English goats' cheese chunks for a great lunch in the British outdoors.

The recipe calls for red watercress, which has just recently been launched here in the UK, but you can substitute green watercress instead if you can't get hold of it.

INGREDIENTS (Serves 4)

2 oranges, peeled, pithed and cut into segments (reserve the juice)

1 head chicory

1 bunch salad onions, cut into lozenges

1 bunch mizuna

1 bunch red watercress

4 radishes, cut into very thin slices

2 tablespoons reserved orange juice

2 teaspoons Dijon mustard

1 tablespoon sherry vinegar

3 tablespoons extra virgin olive oil

To finish
Few pea tops
Few nasturtium flowers
Crispy croutons

METHOD

1. Make the dressing by whisking together the orange juice and dijon mustard. Add the vinegar, then the olive oil, whisk together and season to taste.

2. Prepare the chicory by removing the core from the base, divide into individual leaves then arrange in a bowl.

3. Mix together the mizuna, red watercress, spring onions and radish. Drizzle over ¾ of the dressing and mix together lightly.

4. Place the mizuna mix in the centre of the chicory leaves, scatter over the croutons, orange segments and a drizzle of the remaining dressing and finally a scattering of nasturtium flowers and pea tops.

This is flower-power in a salad

"Your flexible friend — choose what vegetables are in season, and the sauce will go with them. It's a good sauce to master"

ASPARAGUS MILLE FEUILLE WITH SALT AND VINEGAR SAUCE

No, I've not been on the beer again. The salt and vinegar sauce is based on memories of a fish and chip shop, showering the fish with salt and a fantastic zing of vinegar. I've combined the two and put it together into a version of the classic 'Beurre Blanc.' The sauce uses more vinegar and I use salted butter which really enhances the asparagus.

If asparagus is out of season you could substitute with a mixture of chestnut mushrooms or even just some steamed broccoli.

INGREDIENTS *(Serves 4)*

200g puff pastry
1 egg yolk
1 tablespoon olive oil
4 shallots, finely chopped
1 clove garlic, finely chopped
200g young spinach leaves, washed
Pinch ground nutmeg

For the sauce
200ml white wine
250ml white wine vinegar
2 tablespoons whipping cream
200g chilled salted butter, diced
Flesh 1 beef tomato, diced
1 tablespoon chives, chopped
2 bunches of asparagus, peeled and trimmed

METHOD

1. Roll out the puff pastry ¾cm thick and cut into rectangles. Brush with the egg yolk and mark into diamonds.

2. Bake in a hot oven (180°c) for 10 minutes until risen and golden brown.

3. Heat the olive oil and sauté the shallots and garlic together until softened. Add the spinach and wilt. Season to taste with salt, pepper and nutmeg.

4. Place the white wine and vinegar in a pan. Bring to the boil and reduce by half. Stir in the cream and reduce again. Finish with the diced butter a little at a time until the sauce is emulsified.

5. Add the diced tomato and chives and season. Do not boil the sauce or it will separate.

6. Blanch the asparagus in some boiling salted water for 2-3 minutes until al dente.

7. When ready to serve, cut each rectangle in half lengthways. Place the spinach in the base of half of each puff pastry piece. Arrange the asparagus on each one, pour over the sauce and finally top with the reserved lid.

CARROT AND CREAMY LANCASHIRE TIMBALE

A great vegetarian starter or alternatively use as an accompaniment to a piece of poached chicken or roast cod. The salt and vinegar sauce on the previous page also works well with this recipe.

INGREDIENTS *(Makes 4 ramekins)*

50g butter
3 carrots, peeled and grated
2 shallots, finely chopped
1 clove garlic
Small knob fresh root ginger, chopped
100g mashed potato
2 eggs
50g creamy Lancashire cheese
200ml tomato passata
4 leaves fresh basil, shredded
25ml crème fraîche

To serve
A selection of summer vegetables blanched. Fresh peas and broad beans are ideal

METHOD

1. Heat the butter and sweat off the carrots, garlic, shallot and ginger for 5 minutes until softened.

2. Add the potato, eggs and cheese. Mix well and season.

3. Line ramekin dishes with food wrap. Fill with the mixture and cover.

4. Bake in a bain-marie, 180°c for 20 minutes.

5. Heat the passata, basil and crème fraîche.

6. Warm through the vegetables.

7. When ready to serve, place the timbales onto plates and carefully remove moulds. Spoon around the sauce and top with the market vegetables. It's a summer sensation.

"This is one of my 'desert island dishes'
I could eat it all the time"

LANCASHIRE CAULIFLOWER CHEESE

I could eat this morning, lunch or dinner on its own or with a seared steak or roast chicken. Sublime! I read recently that cauliflower sales have declined over recent years, as broccoli increasingly finds favour with buyers instead. But in my view there's no contest when dishes like this are on the menu.

INGREDIENTS
(Serves 6 as a side order)

1 head cauliflower
50g butter
50g flour
500ml milk
150g grated Lancashire cheese
Pinch paprika

To finish
Extra Lancashire cheese
Pinch parmesan cheese, grated

METHOD

1. Steam a whole head of cauliflower until tender then cut into chunks and place in a baking dish.
2. Make a roux by melting the butter and then adding the plain flour. Cook for a minute then slowly add the milk, mixing well. Simmer gently until thickened.
3. Add the cheeses and paprika. Season to taste.
4. Pour over the cauliflower and sprinkle with a little extra cheese and place under a hot grill until golden and bubbling.

HOT DOGS ARE WORTH RELISHING

It was 3am on a chill January morning and I was just leaving the Hog and Heffer night spot in a district that's home to the meat packing industry of New York. I vowed I would never eat one of these mass-manufactured items, but after far too much alcohol, the smell of the frankfurters and sizzling onions was too much to ignore. As they say, when in Rome... and you know what, they were pretty damn good. And yes, I did have more than one.

Taking inspiration from my midnight feast, I thought I'd take this American delight to the next level. First change has to be the sausage - so out goes the frankfurter and in comes a designer sausage from a local butcher. Wildbloods in Norden are regarded as making some of the best in the area. Next the bread, get it as fresh as you can and finally, cap it all with the finest relish. Try this pair.

SPICY ONION AND CORIANDER RELISH

- 1 tablespoon olive oil
- 2 white onions, peeled and sliced fine
- 1 teaspoon caster sugar
- 1 teaspoon dried chilli flakes
- 1 clove garlic
- 1 tablespoon white wine vinegar
- 1 tablespoon coriander chopped

1. Heat the olive oil in a casserole pan and add the onions - cook gently for 10 minutes until softened.
2. Add the sugar, chilli and garlic and continue cooking for a further 2 minutes
3. Remove from the heat, add the vinegar and leave to cool.
4. Stir in the coriander, season and place in fridge until ready to use.

TOMATO AND MUSTARD RELISH

- 1 tablespoon olive oil
- 2 shallots, chopped fine
- 8 plum tomatoes, blanched and flesh diced
- 1 clove garlic, finely chopped
- 1 tablespoon sherry vinegar
- 1 teaspoon Pommery mustard
- 1 tablespoon fresh basil leaves, shredded

1. Heat the olive oil and fry the shallots for 2 minutes until softened.
2. Add the diced tomato and garlic and slowly cook for 20 minutes until all the water has evaporated from the tomatoes.
3. Remove from heat, add vinegar and Pommery mustard and when cool stir in the basil. Season and place in fridge until ready to use.

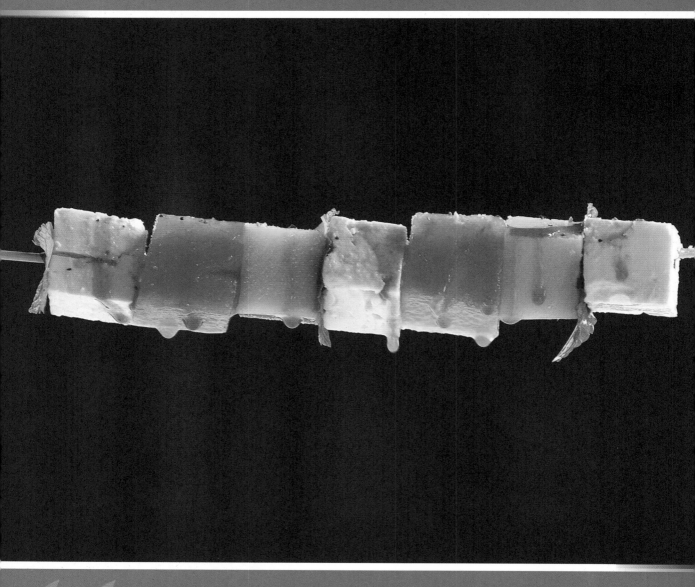

"Forget cheap Cheddar cheese and pineapple on a stick — watermelon and feta is the next big thing!!"

WATERMELON, MANGO AND FETA KEBABS

Take straight out of the fridge so the melon is crisp and juicy. Ideal if you're having a barbecue and waiting for your coals to heat up.

INGREDIENTS *(Makes 10 kebabs)*

1 ripe, seedless watermelon
200g feta cheese
1 ripe mango, peeled
Few sprigs fresh mint
1 tablespoon caster sugar
2 tablespoons white wine vinegar
6 tablespoons olive oil
Salt and freshly ground pepper
Squeeze fresh lemon

METHOD

1. Remove the outer rind of the watermelon and dice the flesh into 2cm cubes. Remove any black pips.

2. Cut the feta and mango into identically-sized cubes.

3. Take a kebab stick and place alternate cubes of the fruits, cheese and the occasional mint leaf onto the stick.

4. Mix together the sugar, vinegar, olive oil and seasoning and pour over each kebab – serve chilled and just before serving finish with a squeeze of lemon.

ASPARAGUS SALAD WITH A HERB AND TOMATO DRESSING

Asparagus is one of those classic vegetables best eaten in May or June while the English varieties are at their best. Great with hollandaise, mayonnaise or even quite simply a tomato, shallot and balsamic vinaigrette.

Two varieties of asparagus are used in this dish. There's green asparagus which is cut above the ground and the white asparagus, which is deprived of light by soil being placed around the stem. The lack of light prevents it from producing chlorophyll and turning green. It results in a more tender but expensive variety.

INGREDIENTS (Serves 4)

1 bunch English asparagus, peeled to just below the tip
1 bunch white asparagus, peeled to just below the tip
2 beef tomatoes, peeled and flesh diced
2 shallots, finely chopped
1 tablespoon chives, chopped
Few leaves fresh basil, shredded
2 tablespoons balsamic vinegar
6 tablespoons olive oil
Juice of ½ lemon

To finish
Sea salt
Cracked black pepper
Fresh herb sprigs
Extra virgin olive oil

METHOD

1. Blanch the asparagus spears in a pan of boiling salted water and cook until al dente – approximately 2-3 minutes depending on thickness. Plunge immediately into ice-cold water.

2. Mix together the tomato chunks, shallots, chives, vinegar, oil and lemon and season to taste – if making in advance, add the herbs at the last minute.

3. Cut the spears, removing any woody bits and arrange on plates. Place the tomato dressing on top and finally scatter on the sea salt, pepper, herbs and drizzle of extra virgin olive oil.

Simple. Stunning. Life can offer few things better than this

CELERIAC REMOULADE

You've barbecued your sausages and burgers, the potato salad is at the ready but what else do you serve with it? To make it a proper meal remoulade is the answer. A fantastic accompaniment to any barbecue meal, it's delicate but with a subtle lemon and mustard kick.

INGREDIENTS (Makes 1 bowl enough for 6 people)

225g celeriac, trimmed and grated
1 carrot, peeled and grated
1 red onion, finely sliced
1 tablespoon sherry vinegar
1 teaspoon caster sugar
1 tablespoon Dijon mustard
4 tablespoons mayonnaise
Lemon juice to taste
Fresh coriander and chives

METHOD

1. In a bowl, mix together the grated celeriac, carrot and red onion.
2. Add the sherry vinegar, sugar and a good pinch of salt and pepper.
3. Mix well then add the mustard and mayonnaise. Add the lemon juice and adjust the seasoning.
4. Finish with coriander and chives.

STUFFED BABY COURGETTES WITH TOMATO AND BASIL CONFIT

After doing my apprenticeship at the Savoy, I ventured over to France for a couple of years. I was working at the Chateau de Montreuil near Le Touquet and every morning I had the job of picking the herbs and vegetables of the day from the restaurant's vegetable garden. At the time it was a pain in the arse but looking back now it gave me more understanding and respect for the products I use in my dishes today.

One of the worst jobs was picking out the courgettes with the flowers intact. The delicate task of peeling back the dense leaves, with dew still lingering on them, was tricky with shaky hands caused by a hangover. But it paled into insignificance compared to the roasting I'd get from the chef if the flowers fell off.

INGREDIENTS *(Serves 4 as a starter or 8 as a side dish)*

For the tomato and basil confit
1 tablespoon olive oil
4 shallots, finely chopped
6 beef tomatoes, blanched and deseeded
2 teaspoons caster sugar
10 leaves fresh basil, shredded
Salt and fresh ground pepper to taste
12 baby courgettes with flowers

For the dressing
2 tablespoons sherry vinegar
6 tablespoons extra virgin olive oil
1 shallot, finely chopped
Squeeze lemon juice

To finish
Fresh basil leaves

METHOD

1. For the tomato confit; heat the olive oil and fry the shallots on a gentle heat for 2-3 minutes to soften.

2. Dice the flesh of the blanched tomatoes, reserving one tablespoon of tomato for the dressing.

3. Add the diced tomato flesh to the shallot mix and cook slowly for approximately 20 minutes until the water in the tomatoes has evaporated and the mixture has condensed to a pulp.

4. Remove from the heat then add the sugar and basil. Season to taste.

5. Place a few teaspoons of the mixture inside each flower. Steam for 3 minutes until hot, but still al dente.

6. Place on your serving dish, mix together the dressing ingredients and the reserved tablespoon of tomato, drizzle over the top, finish with a final flourish of basil leaves and shower with salt and pepper.

Please note - If you can't get hold of the courgettes with their flowers on, just use small courgettes cut into lozenges. Gently fry in olive oil for 2-3 minutes the add the tomato confit and dressing. It won't look as appetising but it will still taste pretty damn fine.

Simple, but just look at the
visual impact

NUTS!
ABOUT DESSERTS

The combination of tastes and textures has to be tried to be believed

BLACKCURRANT CRÈME BRULÉE

A beautiful velvety set cream, crisp on top, sweet from the sugar but tart from the acidic tones of the fruits and the citrus tang of the lemon. What more could you ask for? There, you've got me going all Jilly Goolden.

INGREDIENTS *(Makes 6)*

Zest 1 lemon
1 vanilla pod, split
500ml whipping cream
6 egg yolks
100g caster sugar
Punnet of blackcurrants
Additional sugar for dusting

To serve
Fresh red and blackcurrant sprigs
Fresh mint

METHOD

1. Place the lemon zest, juice, vanilla and cream into a small pan. Bring to a gentle simmer, remove from heat and leave to infuse for 10 minutes.

2. Mix together the egg yolks and sugar. Remove the vanilla pod from the cream and pour onto the egg yolk mixture. Mix until it is all incorporated.

3. Divide the blackcurrants between the ramekin dishes, pour in the cream mixture and place into a bain-marie. Bake in a warm oven (120°c) for approximately 30 minutes until just set. Remove from oven and leave to cool.

4. When ready to serve, dust each ramekin with the extra caster sugar. Caramelise under a hot grill or glaze with a blow torch.

5. Serve on its own or maybe with some blackcurrant sorbet, fruits and almond tuiles.

CHOCOLATE BLANCMANGE

Whatever happened to blancmange? For me it was one of those childhood experiences, eaten hot from a bowl or cold at a birthday party - usually served in the shape of a rabbit with green jelly chopped around to resemble grass.

I've chosen our family recipe, which has been passed down over the years. I value traditions like this as so many of the recipes that are part of our heritage are being lost or forgotten.

Lest the current generation isn't familiar with blancmange, it's a semi-solid dessert similar to custard but thickened with cornflour. It dates back to medieval England when it was actually a savoury dish using all white ingredients. The French then commandeered it as a dessert, and gave it a name – meaning literally "eat white".

INGREDIENTS *(Makes 6)*

600ml milk
1 vanilla pod, split
3 tablespoons caster sugar
4 tablespoons corn flour
125g grated chocolate
1 tablespoon Tia Maria

To finish
50ml whipping cream

METHOD

1. Take 550ml of milk and warm it through with the vanilla pod. Leave for 20 minutes to infuse then add the sugar.

2. Mix the remaining cold milk with the cornflour and pour into the milk mixture. Return to the heat and whisk until thickened and the flour is cooked out.

3. Remove from heat, mix in the chocolate and Tia Maria and pour into serving containers or bowls.

4. Eat either hot or cold with whipping cream poured over and a scattering of fruits.

"Everyone has their own version —
this one has a subtle twist

COX'S APPLE CRUMBLE WITH A WALNUT TOPPING

Here's a classic UK favourite dessert and one of mine as well. Leave this one till the wintery months when the nights are drawing in and it's getting a bit nippy. I serve it with the custard, apple and the crumble mixture all together in individual ramekins. If you really like your custard, go ahead and add more.

In this recipe I use Cox's, the best-known dessert apple. It has a rich, slightly sweet, almost nutty flavour. The skin is occasionally russetted, with autumnal reds and yellows over green. It is perfect for stewing, which makes it magic for crumbles.

INGREDIENTS *(Serves 10)*

For the crumble
50g caster sugar
50g soft brown sugar
25g plain flour
1 teaspoon cinnamon powder
40g walnuts
40g chilled butter

For the apple mixture
25g butter
4 Cox's apples, cored and cut into 1cm dice
50g raisins, soaked overnight in 1 tablespoon rum
0.25 teaspoon cinnamon powder
1 pinch grated nutmeg

For the custard
300ml milk
Vanilla pod, split
2 egg yolks
50g caster sugar
25g plain flour

To serve
Ice cream
Apple crisps

METHOD

1. To make the walnut topping, process together the caster sugar, brown sugar, flour, cinnamon and walnuts in a food processor until finely ground.

2. Add the butter and pulse until it forms a crumb texture.

3. To make the apple filling, heat the butter in a frying pan until nut-brown, then add the apples and fry, tossing lightly, until softened.

4. Add the raisins, cinnamon and nutmeg and mix well. Set aside to cool.

5. To make the custard, heat the milk and vanilla in a saucepan until just beginning to boil.

6. Mix together the yolks and sugar in a bowl, then stir in the flour.

7. Pour half the milk onto the egg mixture, and return to the pan. Simmer until thickened, stirring all the time.

8. Preheat the oven to 180°c. Spoon some of the custard into small ramekins, top with the apple mixture, then scatter some crumble mixture over each ramekin.

9. Bake for 8-10 minutes until the topping is golden. Serve warm with your favourite ice cream and apple crisps.

RASPBERRY ETON MESS

Tradition demands this classic dessert is made with English strawberries. But when Noonie my fruit and veg supplier turned up on my doorstep with a few cases of raspberries to shift, the temptation was too much to resist. And what a superb twist on the standard version it turned out to be.

In its original form, Eton mess is a dessert made by mashing fruits with cream. It has since evolved with additions of crumbled meringue and liqueur.

But wait until you try this version; it's quick, easy, chic and even better finished off with crumbled honeycomb to give it that extra toffee crunch.

INGREDIENTS

2 punnets fresh raspberries
Squeeze fresh lemon
Icing sugar to taste
250ml whipping cream
25g icing sugar
4 meringue nests, crumbled (buy these from your supermarket)
4 tablespoons Grand Marnier

To finish
Additional fruit
Fresh mint
Honeycomb chunks, crumbled (see page 180)

METHOD

1. Take one punnet of raspberries and liquidise to a purée. Pass through a sieve, then add the lemon and icing sugar to taste.

2. Whisk the whipping cream and sugar together until it forms soft peaks

3. Take 4 martini glasses and arrange some of the raspberries in the base. Drizzle over the Grand Marnier then spoon on alternate layers of the raspberry coulis, crumbled meringue and whipped cream to create a layered trifle look.

4. Finish with some more whole fruit, mint and a showering of honeycomb.

*Of course it's messy to eat
— do you care?*

CRÈME BRÛLÉE CRUNCH

Cast the mind back to childhood for the moment. Concentrate, and you can almost taste that ice-cream sandwich at the seaside. One wave of the Nutter magic wand and those soggy wafers of past times are replaced by crisp brandy snap.

One more and the synthetic ice cream becomes a set pure vanilla custard. Don't even use a spoon for this one. Take the dessert in both hands, raise to the mouth, bite. Ahh! Silence is golden.

INGREDIENTS *(Serves 10)*

For the crème brulée
500ml whipping cream
1 vanilla pod, split in half
6 egg yolks
85g caster sugar

To serve
Brandy snap wafers (see page 188)
Selection of fresh fruits, possibly including; mango, pineapple, apple and berries
Sprig fresh mint

For the frosted grapes (as an additional extra)
1 bunch grapes
2 egg whites
100g coloured sherbet

METHOD

1. Place the cream into a pan, scrape the seeds from the vanilla and add to the cream along with the pod itself. Bring to the boil then remove from the heat.

2. Mix together the egg yolks and sugar and stir in the hot cream. Remove the vanilla pod and then pour into 6 ramekin dishes.

3. Place the dishes in a Bain Marie and bake in an oven (120°c) for about 40 minutes until set. Remove from the oven and leave to cool. Place in fridge until ready to use.

4. For the brandy snap wafers follow the method on page 188 but instead of shaping them whilst still warm, leave them flat. These can be made ahead and left in an airtight container until ready to use.

5. For the frosted grapes, pick the grapes from the stem, toss in the egg whites then roll in the sherbet to cover them. Leave for 2-3 hours to get crusty.

6. When ready to serve the crème brulée crunch, slice the fresh fruits, arrange on individual plates and place a brandy snap on top. Un-mould the cooked custards carefully by running a knife around the rim of each dish and give it a good shake. Place each custard on top of the brandy snap and top each one with another snap to form a designer sandwich.

7. Scatter with the frosted grapes and sprig of mint.

LIQUORICE ICE CREAM

Delving amongst the many jars of so-called childhood treats in the shop window of a local sweetshop, I experienced a variety of tastes and textures that took me back to when I were nobbut a lad. Foremost among them was the Pontefract cake, a liquorice button made from an extract of the liquorice root. The extract is also used to flavour the classic liqueur Sambuca. No wonder I love it so much.

If you enjoyed the Pontefract cakes, take it to the next level with strawberry liquorice sticks. The end result is quite simply stunning...an almost strawberry milkshake/bubblegum taste with a subtle tone of that Sambuca flavouring.

INGREDIENTS *(Makes ½ litre of ice cream)*

- 400ml milk
- 100ml whipping cream
- 1 vanilla pod, split
- 4 egg yolks
- 100g caster sugar
- 100g Pontefract cakes
- 2 tablespoons water

METHOD

1. Warm the milk, cream and vanilla together and bring to a light simmer. Remove from the heat and leave to infuse for 20 minutes.

2. Mix together the egg yolks and sugar, remove the vanilla pod from the milk mixture and re-boil. Pour half the mixture onto the eggs and mix well, then return the whole lot back to the remaining milk in the pan.

3. Return the pan to the stove and place over a gentle heat, stirring at all times until it coats the back of a spoon. Remove from the heat and pass through a sieve.

4. Over a bain-marie heat the Pontefract cakes and water and stir until the cakes have melted to a purée (have patience as it takes about 10 minutes to melt). Stir into the custard mixture.

5. When you are ready to freeze the ice cream, place in an ice cream maker and follow the guidelines for your particular machine to freeze and churn, place in the freezer for 30 minutes to firm.

6. Scoop when desired and enjoy!!

"OK, so Pontefract's in Yorkshire. But only Lancastrians could have thought of putting their most famous product in ice cream"

TREACLE TART WITH ORANGE AND PECAN SALAD

A utumn is well and truly upon us the clocks have gone back, the nights are drawing in and the leaves are falling from the trees. The mind turns to treacle tart, comfort food at its hot, sticky, gooey best. It's perfect with vanilla custard, a dollop of mascarpone or quite simply with a ball of ice cream. If you can't get the dry breadcrumbs, use fresh but add more syrup otherwise it gets a bit gloopy.

The tarts can be made in advance and left in the fridge. Warm them through for about 3-4 minutes at 180°C to get them hot again.

INGREDIENTS *(Serves 6)*

For the pastry
110g butter
50g caster sugar
1 egg yolk
175g plain flour, sifted
Pinch salt
Few drops vanilla essence

For the filling
250g golden syrup
Zest and juice 1 lemon
250g dry white breadcrumbs
1 egg
Few drops vanilla essence

For the orange salad
2 oranges
50g sliced pecan nuts
Juice ½ lemon
50g sugar
Chocolate transfer decoration (optional)
Vanilla ice cream

METHOD

1. Cream the butter and sugar together, add the egg and beat well. Beat in the flour, salt and vanilla. Cover in food wrap and leave in a fridge for 20 minutes before using. Line 6 10cm in diameter tart tins with the pastry and bake at 180°c for 8 minutes until a light golden colour.

2. Warm the golden syrup so it becomes easier to stir and mix in the lemon zest and juice, breadcrumbs, egg and vanilla essence.

3. Pour into the baked pastry cases and bake in a hot oven (180°c) for 8-10 minutes until a light golden colour. Leave to cool.

4. For the orange salad; segment the oranges, place the orange juices, lime juice and sugar into a small pan and bring to the boil to form a light syrup. Leave to cool then pour over the segments and add the pecans.

5. When ready to serve, either reheat the tart briefly or serve at room temperature with the orange salad, chocolate decoration, ice cream and a dusting of icing sugar.

NUTTER'S STICKY CHRISTMAS PUDDING

Christmas wouldn't be Christmas without a Christmas pudding but a lot of people find it too heavy and rich and after a couple of spoonfuls they're beaten. Nutter to the rescue! This dessert brings together all the tastes and flavours of your traditional pudding but is so light, fluffy and gooey that it's the perfect finale to any festive feast.

INGREDIENTS *(Serves 4)*

180ml water
125g pitted dates
½ lemon, grated zest and juiced
½ orange, grated zest and juiced
a few drops of vanilla flavouring
2 teaspoons Camp coffee
6 teaspoons bicarbonate of soda
90g butter
4 eggs
50g walnuts, chopped
200g self-raising flour
125g mincemeat
100g glacé cherries, halved
1 teaspoon cinnamon
Pinch of mixed spice

For the clementine sugar
100g sugar
2 clementines, zest only

For the sauce
230g caster sugar
4 tablespoons water
12 tablespoons whipping cream
100g butter
100g mincemeat

To serve
Hazelnuts dipped in liquid caramel

METHOD

1. Preheat the oven to 150°c.
2. Simmer the water and the dates together in a pan for 10 minutes.
3. Add the lemon and orange zest, vanilla flavouring, Camp coffee and bicarbonate of soda, and blend in a food processor until smooth.
4. Make the clementine sugar by blending together the sugar and clementine zest in a food processor until well mixed.
5. In a mixing bowl, cream together the clementine sugar and butter.
6. Mix in the eggs, add the walnuts, flour, mincemeat, cherries, cinnamon and mixed spice, mixing well, then combine with the date mixture.
7. Pour into a greased roasting tray and bake for 25 minutes until spongy. Allow to cool slightly.
8. Meanwhile, make the sauce. Boil the sugar and water together in a pan until it caramelises, turning golden brown.
9. Stir in the cream and butter, then add the mincemeat.
10. To serve, cut out 4 individual rounds of the sponge pudding. Spoon over the sauce and serve with your favourite ice cream and hazelnut sugar strands.

RASPBERRY RATAFIA TRIFLE

Ratafia is a sweet, brandy-based liqueur flavoured with fruit or almonds. Popular in Victorian times, nowadays it is commonly associated with Ratafia biscuits - small, crunchy biscuits flavoured with bitter almond and similar to a macaroon. In this recipe I have substituted the usual sponge finger in a trifle with the ratafia biscuits, which give the dessert a fantastic almond crunch.

INGREDIENTS *(Serves 6)*

For the custard
600ml milk
1 teaspoon orange zest
4 egg yolks
115g caster sugar
55g plain flour

For the cream
450ml whipping cream, whipped
2 tablespoons icing sugar
Few drops of vanilla essence
1 packet Ratafia biscuits
2 fl oz rum or amaretto liquor
2 punnets raspberries

METHOD

1. For the custard, heat the milk with the orange until simmering. Mix together the egg yolks and sugar then add the flour and mix well. Pour half the milk into the egg mixture, mixing well, then pour back into the remaining milk in the pan. Return to the heat and cook for approx 1 minute until thick and creamy. Remove from heat and leave to cool.

2. Whisk together the whipping cream, icing sugar and vanilla until it forms soft peaks.

3. To construct your trifles, break up some Ratafia biscuits in the bottom of 6 martini glasses. Drizzle over some of the rum and then make a layer of custard, followed by layers of raspberries, whipped cream, more biscuits, custard, fruit and cream until you have a fabulous layered glass. Refrigerate until ready to serve.

VANILLA POACHED PEARS

Sometimes simplicity rules. The juicy white flesh of the pear is sheer heaven when eaten at perfect ripeness. This recipe calls for Rocha Pears but if the only ones available aren't ripe, just choose a different variety instead.

The Rocha Pear is medium-sized and has a slight brownish neck. Its yellow skin is dotted with brown and green and its flesh is soft and buttery when ripe. I feel poaching them brings out their natural sweetness. Peel just before cooking and sprinkle with lemon juice to stop the flesh oxidising.

INGREDIENTS *(Serves 4)*

300g caster sugar
500ml water
250ml dry white wine
1 vanilla pod, split
1 lemon, cut in half
1 stick of cinnamon
6 Rocha pears, peeled and cored but with stalks attached
150g mascarpone cheese
Fresh mint
Vanilla ice cream

METHOD

1. Place the sugar, water, wine, vanilla, lemon and cinnamon in a pan and bring to the boil.
2. Place in the pears upright in the liquid then cover and poach very gently until tender, for about 25 minutes.
3. Leave to cool in the syrup then place in the fridge.
4. When ready to serve, take each pear and use the mascarpone to fill the hole left after removal of the core.
5. Place the pears on a serving plate, scatter with fresh mint and a drizzle of the cooking liquor and a scoop of ice cream if desired.

"Here's the secret of how to create a winning dish from an everyday fruit"

" A chilled out treat with
raspberries or strawberries "

RASPBERRY & STRAWBERRY SORBET

S orbet is classically the ultimate palate cleanser in between courses of a grand dinner, or more so now as a refreshing dessert at the end of a meal. It's simply a water-based ice made without dairy products or egg yolks, but some recipes do contain egg whites. When I make sorbet I first pick out the fruits that are slightly overripe – if you're going to purée them, it makes sense.

Don't like raspberries? Just replace the same quantity of raspberries with strawberries in the recipe and hey presto, strawberry sorbet.

INGREDIENTS *(Makes around 1 litre)*

For the raspberry sorbet

375ml stock syrup
(Made by dissolving 250g sugar in 250ml water with half a vanilla pod in a pan. Bring to the boil then remove from the heat and leave to infuse until cool.)
450g raspberries
Juice of 2 lemons

METHOD

1. To make the sorbet, place the cool stock syrup in a food processor. Add the raspberries and lemon and blend to a pulp. Pass through a sieve.

2. Place in an ice cream machine and churn according to the machine's guidelines until smooth and firm. Serve straight away or place in the freezer. Try and eat within a few days otherwise it will lose its smooth consistency and ice crystals will form.

WHITE CHOCOLATE AND STRAWBERRY FUDGE CHEESECAKE

What more could one ask for. Its chocoholic heaven, the strawberry chocolate so reminds me of those pink panther bars back in my childhood. Its rich, decadent and quite simply sublime.

INGREDIENTS *(Serves 10)*

For the base
400g custard cream biscuits, crushed
100g melted butter

For the cheesecake mix
500g mascarpone cream cheese
50g caster sugar
350ml whipping cream, whipped
350g white chocolate, melted

For the topping
75g caster sugar
375ml whipping cream
175g strawberry coloured and flavoured chocolate
75g butter

To serve
Chocolate transfer sheets
Seasonal fruits

METHOD

1. For the base – mix together the crushed biscuits and butter. Press into a 20cm x 15cm tray lined with cling film.

2. Gently mix together the mascarpone and sugar, fold in the whipped cream then quickly fold in the melted chocolate. Spoon on top of the biscuits. Refrigerate.

3. For the topping – boil the sugar and cream together and simmer for 8 minutes or until a pale yellow colour, mix in the chocolate and butter, cool slightly then top the cheesecake with the mixture. Leave to set for about 3 hours in the fridge.

4. When ready to serve turn out of the tray and slice, with a warm knife, into rectangular pieces. Decorate with the seasonal fruit and chocolate transfers.

A real chocoholics treat!!

(n)UTS!
ABOUT SWEET TREATS

" So easy a child could make it.
They'd spend the rest of the time
fighting off the adults "

RED BANANA CHOC ICE

Red bananas are smaller and plumper than the traditional yellow variety. Their texture is slightly softer and the flavour is that of a beautiful raspberry banana cream. If you can't get hold of their Brazilian cousins, small yellow bananas will do.

INGREDIENTS *(Serves 4)*

2 hands mini red bananas
300g dark chocolate, melted
100g white chocolate, melted

Optional
Mixed chopped nuts
Pouring cream

METHOD

1. Skin the bananas, pat dry with a paper towel then dip carefully in the dark chocolate. Shake off any excess and place on a sheet of non-stick baking parchment.

2. Leave to set then place the white chocolate into a piping bag. Drizzle over the chocolate bananas then leave to set.

3. Serve as they are or scatter with chopped nuts and pouring cream. Or for something different, place in the freezer and you have an instant banana choc ice.

CHERRY LOAF

G lacé cherries aren't everyone's cup of tea but I love them, especially when they break down as they are simmered and turn the batter deliciously sweet and a glorious pink colour.

INGREDIENTS *(Makes 1 loaf tin)*

225g glacé cherries
300ml milk
250g caster sugar
175g butter
350g self raising flour
2 eggs

To finish
3 tablespoons Kirsch

METHOD

1. Place the glacé cherries in a casserole pan and add the milk, caster sugar and butter.

2. Bring to the boil, stirring occasionally, and simmer for 4 minutes. Remove from the heat and leave to cool.

3. Add the flour and eggs and beat well.

4. Pour into a greased and lined loaf tin and bake in a hot oven (180°c) for 10 minutes. Reduce the temperature to 150°c and continue cooking for 30 minutes more.

5. Remove from the oven and leave to cool. Drizzle over the Kirsch then wrap in food wrap. Store in an airtight container until you fancy a nibble.

Available at all good sweet shops, or your nearest 3-star Michelin restaurant

MARSHMALLOW

One of my favourite childhood munchies is suddenly back in vogue. Gordon Ramsay makes vanilla; I make mint and also a savoury one with black olive and parmesan. But the best has to be lavender-scented ones at the 3 star Michelin Restaurant Le Louis XV in Monaco; they are pulled out of a glass bon-bon jar, these foot-long tubes of lilac confection, and then cut into flumps with the aid of silver pincers – awesome.

INGREDIENTS

32g leaf gelatine
8 tablespoons of water
500g icing sugar
50g glucose
170ml water
2 egg whites
Few drops of rosewater
100g cornflour
100g icing sugar

METHOD

1. Soak gelatine in water for about 10 minutes until softened.

2. In a pan, bring the icing sugar, glucose and water to the boil and simmer for 4 minutes. Remove from the heat and stir in the soaked gelatine.

3. Place the egg whites into the bowl, whisk with an electric mixer and as you do so add the hot syrup. Continue to whisk on high speed for 10 minutes then add the flavouring and colouring.

4. Line a tray with cling film and dust with cornflour and icing sugar. Add the cooled marshmallow, and then dust again with more cornflour and sugar.

5. Leave to cool completely, slice into rectangles, dust again with cornflour and sugar.

CLASSIC HONEYCOMB

Watch out for children over-indulging on these fabulous sweet treats as they're an instant sugar rush and they'll be running around like headless chickens. Eat on their own, dip in hot chocolate sauce or even crumble and scatter over ice cream. Either way they are sure to impress.

INGREDIENTS

325g caster sugar
50g honey
125g liquid glucose
60ml water
15g bicarbonate of soda

METHOD

1. In a large heavy bottom pan place the sugar, honey, glucose and water. Bring to the boil and simmer for about 5 minutes until it turns a light toffee colour.

2. Remove from the heat immediately and add the bicarbonate of soda, quickly whisk in then leave to grow. The mixture will treble in size so be careful it doesn't spill out everywhere.

3. Pour out onto a silicone mat and leave to cool.

4. When cool break into chunks, package or store in an airtight container until you fancy a nibble.

"Sweet, bubbly and irresistible. The honeycomb, not me

FRUIT CAKE

Always a firm favourite on our Afternoon Tea selection, it has a great dense fruit flavour with a subtle punch from the brandy and rum. More tea vicar?

INGREDIENTS *(Makes 1 loaf tin)*

For the fruit mixture
40g dried apricots, chopped
40g glacé cherries
40g candid peel
110g sultanas
110g raisins
90g currants
1 tablespoon treacle
Pinch mixed spice
Pinch cinnamon
Zest ½ lemon
Zest ½ orange
50ml brandy

For the cake batter
75g butter
75g soft brown sugar
2 eggs
75g plain flour

To serve
100ml rum
100ml brandy

METHOD

1. Mix together all the fruit mixture ingredients and leave to soak overnight.

2. Cream together the butter and sugar. Add the eggs and mix together until smooth. Mix in the flour then stir in all the marinated fruits.

3. Butter a loaf tin and line with parchment paper. Spoon the mixture into the tin and level with a spatula.

4. Pre-heat an oven to 180°c, bake the loaf for 10 minutes then reduce the temperature to 140°c and bake for a further 45 minutes.

5. Remove from oven and leave to cool.

6. Turn out of the tin and douse in the rum and brandy. Wrap in food wrap and leave for a week to mature.

7. Serve in 1cm thick slices.

CLASSIC FRUIT TARTS

Fruit tarts were always a favourite of mine. They take me back to my days when as a teenager working in France, I'd pass by the village patisserie and ogle at the sheer array of cream cakes, tarts and gateaux – the strawberry tart being the ultimate prize in the window.

Sadly over here such delights are scarce. It's mainly the territory of the supermarkets, which produce their own versions, lacking the finesse and chic of the classic French patisseries. So forget the Eurostar ride to Paris – make these at home, get your chequered table cloth out, don a beret and stick on an 'Allo 'Allo DVD.

Once you've made your pastry cases, it's on to an onerous decision of what filling and fruit to use.

I've included a few of my favourites – the classic crème patissiere, a zingy lemon curd and a light and airy crème Chantilly.

If making these tarts in advance, brush the insides with melted dark chocolate. When it is set, fill with the filling of choice then decorate with your desired fruit.

FOR THE SWEET PASTRY

250g plain flour
90g icing sugar
120g butter
1 egg
Pinch lemon zest

1. In a food processor, blend together the flour, sugar and butter until it forms a fine crumb. Add the egg and lemon and knead to a smooth dough. Place in the fridge to firm up slightly.

2. Lightly dust a work surface with some plain flour. Roll out the pastry thinly to about 2mm thick. Use to line 6 tart cases or alternatively make one large one.

3. Bake in a hot oven (180°c) for about 5 minutes until lightly coloured and golden. Remove from the oven and leave to cool.

CRÈME PATISSIERE

300ml milk
1 vanilla pod, split into half lengthways
2 egg yolks
55g caster sugar
30g plain flour, sifted
Dusting icing sugar
25g dark chocolate, grated

1. For the Crème Patissiere (sounds posh, but in fact it's just classic custard) heat the milk and vanilla together to a gentle simmer then remove from the heat and leave for 20 minutes to infuse.

2. Mix together the egg yolks and sugar then add the flour and mix well. Pour half the milk into the egg mix, then pour this into the remaining milk in the pan. Place on a medium heat and bring to the boil and cook out for 1 minute, stirring well. Pour into a bowl and dust with a touch of icing sugar to prevent a skin forming. Leave to cool.

Strasberry Tart... well worth the effort if you can find them

LEMON CURD

3 egg yolks
2 eggs
75g caster sugar
95g lemon juice
60g butter

1. Whisk together the eggs and sugar.

2. In a saucepan, melt the butter and lemon juice and bring to the boil. Add the egg mixture and simmer for 2-3 minutes, whisking all the time until smooth and thickened.

3. Remove from the heat and leave to cool.

CRÈME CHANTILLY

300ml whipping cream
Seeds from 1 vanilla pod
2 tablespoons icing sugar, sifted
1 tablespoon Grand Marnier (optional)

1. In a chilled mixing bowl, whisk together the cream, vanilla and icing sugar until it forms soft peaks.

2. Add the Grand Marnier and whisk a fraction more.

THE STRASBERRY

Originally a wild strawberry species, the berry was on the verge of extinction before a Dutch grower rediscovered it 7 years ago. This fruit has the genetic makeup of a strawberry, but also tastes like a raspberry. Awesome!

A veritable waltz for the tastebuds

VIENNESE FINGERS

These pretty biscuits make the ideal accompaniment to a steaming hot cuppa! Viennese fingers are classic tea-time treats that are great for sharing, or to nibble on during a break from a hectic day. They are easy to create and are sure to be a crowd pleaser. You'll love the crumbly texture and melt in the mouth buttery taste!

INGREDIENTS

55g icing sugar
225g butter
225g plain flour
Few drops vanilla essence
Dark chocolate, melted

METHOD

1. Cream the butter and icing sugar together then add the flour and vanilla essence and mix well.

2. Put the mixture into a piping bag and pipe the fingers on to a non-stick tray or parchment paper.

3. Bake slowly at 150°c for about 15 minutes until golden brown.

4. Leave to cool then drizzle with melted dark chocolate.

BRANDY SNAP ICE CREAM CONES

orget soggy wafer ice cream cones. These dainty little creations are in a different league – they're crispy, crunchy and irresistible filled with whatever flavour ice cream or sorbet you fancy. I have to admit I am a bit partial to a mint choc chip Cornetto - the ones with dark chocolate at the bottom of each cone.

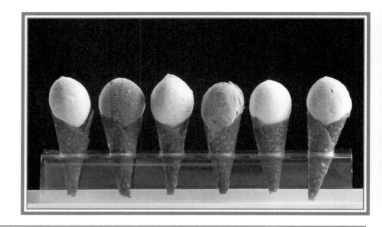

INGREDIENTS

For the brandy snap
100g butter
90g glucose
130g caster sugar
90g plain flour

To serve
Your favourite ice cream

METHOD

1. Melt the butter and glucose together in a small pan. Remove from heat and add the sugar and flour. Mix well.
2. Cool and leave in fridge until needed.
3. To bake, form the mixture into small balls the size of marbles. Place on a non-stick tray well spaced apart and bake in a hot oven 170°c until a light golden colour.
4. Working quickly, lift off the tray and form into cone shapes, leave to cool. Speed is of the essence as the mixture soon goes brittle. Store in an airtight container until ready to use.
5. Spoon your favourite ice cream in the centre and serve.

LEMON POSSET

A fabulous delicate but zingy dessert. Either make in miniature glasses or serve in larger Martini glasses with a scattering of summer fruits and berries doused in limoncello if desired.

INGREDIENTS *(Makes 20 miniature glasses)*

570ml whipping cream
155g caster sugar
Juice of 2 lemons

To finish
100ml whipping cream
2 teaspoons dark and white chocolate, grated
Sprig mint
Sugar decoration

METHOD

1. Place the cream and sugar into a pan and bring to the boil.

2. Boil for 3 minutes then remove from the heat and whisk in the lemon juice.

3. Pour into glasses and leave to set in fridge for a good 6 hours.

4. When ready to serve pipe the whipping cream on top and then shower with the dark and white chocolate.

nuts!
ABOUT ENTERTAINING

THE NUTTER COCKTAIL

S o forget paying high prices, experiment yourself and try this magical creation, it's lavish and quite simply divine. Be warned, one leads to another and they are very high in alcohol, so please drink responsibly. Yeah right, Hic!!

INGREDIENTS *(Makes 1 Glass)*

10ml Grenadine syrup
50ml Red Bull energy drink or equivalent
50ml Champagne
10ml Blavod Vodka

METHOD

1. Pour each drink slowly and carefully over the back of a cocktail spoon into a champagne flute and serve with a sprig of mint and seasonal fruits.

2. Be sure to pour each ingredient in the order stated to get the multi-layered effect.

VOODOO OLIVES

Over the past few years I've demonstrated regularly at the South African Food Festivals in Cape Town, Durban and Johannesburg. Hey, someone has to do these working trips. The thing that impresses me most about the country is the sheer diversity of food and also the people you meet.

Two restaurateurs spring to mind straight away. Marcelle and Sean run the hip and trendy Café 1999 restaurant in Durban. We gelled straight away, not least because we share the same passion for food and Tequila.

They serve these exquisite little olives filled with ricotta cheese as appetisers at the restaurant. Ok on their own, great after one shot of Tequila and they taste totally awesome after six.

If you want an alternative to ricotta do as I do and use a creamy goats cheese instead.

INGREDIENTS (Makes 40 skewers)

100g Rosary goats cheese from Salisbury.
(Alternatively use any creamy goats cheese or try Café 1999's ricotta version)
1 tablespoon chopped chives
Squeeze lemon juice
Dash Tabasco sauce
40 large pitted olives
55g plain flour
1 egg
55g breadcrumbs
Vegetable oil for frying

METHOD

1. Mix together the goats cheese, chives, lemon and Tabasco sauce. Season to taste.

2. Place the cheese mixture into a piping bag with a small nozzle and pipe the goats cheese into each olive.

3. Roll the olives in the flour first, then roll in the egg and finally toss in the breadcrumbs.

4. Heat the olive oil to 180°c and deep-fat fry the olives until a light golden colour.

5. Serve straight away on skewers and insert into voodoo doll (doesn't everyone have one in their bottom drawer?)

"Just the thing for a starter at your dinner party. And you'll actually get time to talk to the guests"

PARMA HAM, PEAR AND GOATS CHEESE TERRINE

A fabulous combination of cheese, ham and fruit. It's ideal if you are entertaining. This terrine can be made the day before and kept in the fridge. To get a perfect slice, place in the freezer for an hour to properly chill, then cut into 1cm thick slices before placing on your serving plates. Allow to rise to room temperature before serving.

INGREDIENTS *(Serves 10)*

2 tablespoons olive oil
2 shallots, finely chopped
2 cloves garlic, chopped
800g rosary goats cheese – (this cheese is mega. It's from Salisbury but can be found at many leading department stores or delicatessens. It has a dense, almost cream cheese type of texture with a wonderful flavour. If you can't get hold of rosary use a good firm cream cheese instead).
2 comice pears, peeled, cored, then poached in stock syrup for about 15 minutes until tender.
1 tablespoon chives, chopped
squeeze lemon
10 slices good quality Parma ham

For the pear purée
2 comice pears, peeled and cored
Pinch sugar
1 teaspoon amaretto
20g butter

To serve
Toasted bread croutes
Mixed baby leaves

METHOD

1. Heat the olive oil in a saucepan and fry the shallots and garlic together over a low light for about 5 minutes until softened but with no colour. Leave to cool.

2. In a mixing bowl, crumble the goats cheese and add the cooled shallot mixture. Dice the pear into small chunks and add along with the chives and lemon. Mix together then season to taste.

3. Line a loaf tin or a triangular terrine mould with cling film. Lay the Parma ham in the tin, overlapping each slice and leaving some to overhang the top.

4. Add the goats cheese mixture and push down well into the corners and sides. Fold over the surplus Parma ham so the cheese is covered. Place in the fridge and leave to chill until ready to use.

5. For the pear purée, take the pears and roughly chop. Place in a dry pan with the amaretto and sugar. Cover with cling film then place on a low light. Leave for 20 minutes until the pear is softened and mushy.

6. Remove from heat, drain off any excess liquid then place in a food processor with the butter and blend to a purée. Season to taste.

7. When ready to serve, slice the terrine and serve with some mixed leaves, crispy croutes and a swoosh of pear purée.

LOBSTER CAESAR SALAD

A stag party is one of life's events that has charted new territory in recent years. Whereas it once amounted to a night in Blackpool, now these jaunts last for days. And more often than not, the destination takes the groom and his henchmen to foreign parts – witness my recent trip to Barcelona.

A man has options in these cases. On the one hand, wear a sombrero, consume several cases of dubious lager, ride along the baggage carousel at the airport, strip naked except for a carefully-positioned sombrero and run around the hotel, nod off over the evening meal and flirt with the Spanish waitress who, you believe with unshakeable conviction, will take up your slurred offer to drop by the next time she's in Preston. Then there is option two. Find a beautiful location and savour some fabulous food and wine. And so it was in Barcelona. Seafood restaurants were right by the port and live lobsters were in abundance. So with influences from the trip I bring you this lobster extravaganza.

This dish is ideal for a pre BBQ appetizer. It's delicate, light and moreish.

Lobster is classed as a luxury food, but a little goes a long way. After making this dish keep the shell and place it in your freezer and when you have 4 lobster shells make the lobster bisque on the next page.

INGREDIENTS (Serves 4)

For the dressing
1 egg yolk
1 clove garlic, crushed
1 tablespoon white wine vinegar
1 tablespoon Dijon mustard
100ml vegetable oil
100ml olive oil
Warm water

For the salad
2 cos lettuce
1 fresh live lobster, cooked for 11 minutes
2 tablespoons croutons
25g parmesan cheese peeled into shavings

METHOD

1. With the help of a hand blender liquidise the egg yolk, garlic, vinegar and Dijon mustard.

2. Mix together the two oils then pour in gradually until the dressing emulsifies and is a light mousse-like consistency. If the mixture goes too stiff thin it out with a touch of warm water.

3. Remove the flesh from the lobster tail, claws and knuckles and slice into medallions.

4. Cut the cos lettuce into bite-size pieces, place in a mixing bowl and add the parmesan, lobster and croutons, then add just enough dressing to coat the leaves with a gentle layer.

5. Season with salt and freshly ground pepper and serve straight away so it remains crisp.

Here's one liaison that's far from dangerous. It helps create this classic among soups

NUTTER'S LOBSTER BISQUE

Lobster bisque is one of the classics of the soup world. This particular recipe originates from London's Savoy Hotel where I did my training when I was 16. It's a rich shellfish broth made with wine, stock and cognac, but, in the Savoy's own decadent style, is finished with a liaison.

A liaison is a mix of egg yolk and cream which is added to the soup just before serving, it thickens it slightly but the overall effect is it gives the soup a silky smooth taste which is just amazing.

INGREDIENTS *(Serves 4)*

1 tablespoon olive oil
Reserved shell of 4 lobsters from the previous recipe, thawed out and crushed with a rolling pin
1 tablespoon tomato purée
2 measures brandy
200ml white wine
100ml Noilly Prat
1 stick of celery, roughly chopped
1 onion, roughly chopped
1 carrot, roughly chopped
1 small fennel, roughly chopped
1 sprig rosemary
1200ml chicken stock

For the liaison
2 egg yolks
200ml cream

To finish
Swirl of crème fraîche
Lobster crostini - optional extra

METHOD

1. In a casserole pan heat the olive oil and fry the crushed lobster bones until toasted, add the tomato purée and then add the brandy, flame it to burn off the alcohol then add the white wine and Noilly Prat.

2. Add the chopped vegetables, rosemary and the chicken stock, bring to the boil and simmer for 40 minutes.

3. Remove from the heat and pass through a sieve, return back to a pan and bring back to the boil.

4. Mix together the egg yolks and cream (the liaison) and pour into the bisque, whisk it in but do not let the soup boil otherwise it will curdle. Season to taste.

5. Pour into warmed bowls and finish with a swirl of crème fraîche. As this is a particularly rich soup, remember to serve smaller portions.

NUTTER'S PARFAIT EXTRAVAGANZA

T his fabulous Chicken Liver Parfait is simple to make and can be transformed into the ultimate dinner party showpiece. It's a dish that always makes me chuckle when it leaves the kitchen. The caperberry sways as it's served, to the delight of all. Pointless I know, but so so quirky.

It was originally designed for a customer who wanted to propose to his girlfriend. Usually we would do something with a ring at the end of the meal but he wanted to get it over and done with so he could enjoy the evening.

So I created this just for them. The only problem for me was that they then wanted it for their wedding reception – for 120 people.

INGREDIENTS *(Serves 10)*

4 shallots, finely chopped
50ml port
50ml Madeira
1 clove garlic
2 sprigs rosemary
700g chicken livers
3 teaspoons salt
1 teaspoon cracked black pepper
7 eggs
700g butter, melted and kept warm

For the herb butter
100g soft butter
1 tablespoon chopped chives

To finish
Deep-fried spaghetti
10 caperberries
Blanched chives
Toasted brioche

METHOD

1. Place the shallots, port, Madeira, garlic and rosemary in a pan and simmer for five minutes.
2. Remove from the heat. Add the chicken livers and blend to a smooth paste in a liquidiser.
3. Add the salt, pepper and eggs and blend.
4. Add the butter and blend again.
5. Pass the whole mixture through a fine sieve.
6. Line a terrine mould with food wrap (in my case I've used a specialist triangular mould) and pour the parfait mixture in. Cover with some lightly buttered tin foil and place in a bain-marie then cook in a hot oven (160°c) for approximately 40 minutes until just firm.
7. Remove from oven and leave to cool. Place in fridge overnight.
8. For the herb butter, mix together the soft butter and chives.
9. Remove the parfait from the terrine mould, remove the food wrap and trim off and firm outer edges.
10. Smear the butter over 3 of the sides of the parfait and place in the fridge to set. Then turn over and butter the remaining side. Place back in the fridge to firm.
11. When ready to serve, slice with a warm knife, spike each slice with 4 spaghetti pieces, tie each caperberry with the blanched chive and wrap around the top. Serve with your favourite chutney and some toasted brioche or hot bread.

The roast beef of old England meets
the best of France

ROAST RIB OF BEEF WITH BOUQUETIERE OF VEGETABLES

Once in a while it's worth a blowout especially when you are cooking a family feast. This fits the bill. Try and shop locally for your beef, asking your butcher for assistance if needed.

The Bouquetiere of vegetables is traditionally a French term meaning to garnish or 'bouquet' with an assortment of fresh vegetables. A whole variety of colours, textures and taste are used to give a whole array of flavours. Try and use the vegetables that are in season - they taste better and are also cheaper as well.

INGREDIENTS (Serves 10)

Joint of aged rib of beef, around 3-4 ribs weighing about 4kg
4 tablespoons olive oil
Good grinding of cracked black pepper and sea salt
6 cloves garlic, crushed
1 tablespoon thyme, chopped
1 tablespoon rosemary, chopped

METHOD

1. Take the joint of beef and smear with olive oil. Season heavily, then place in a pre-heated oven (220°c) for 35 minutes until golden.

2. Reduce the temperature to 180°c and cook for a further 20 minutes. With 5 minutes remaining toss the garlic, thyme and rosemary into the cooking juices and then baste over the beef.

3. Remove from the oven, cover in tin foil and leave for 20 minutes to rest.

4. In that time cook and arrange your chosen selection of vegetables and potatoes.

5. Get your carving knife out, slice, serve and crack open a decent bottle of red. You can't go wrong.

ROAST RACK OF LAMB WITH GINGERED LEEKS AND PORT REDUCTION

I so love lamb chops, particularly now I buy proper ones. I say this as my dad was a butcher and a very thrifty one at that. So the Nutter family was fed not the best lamb chops for their tea but the scrawny end ones that customers didn't really want. As kids we didn't know any different so we just ate them. But not any more. I demand the best.

INGREDIENTS (Serves 2)

Few sprigs thyme and rosemary, chopped
2 cloves garlic, finely chopped
1 dessertspoon salt
1 teaspoon cracked black pepper
1 tablespoon olive oil
1 rack of lamb (approx 600g in weight), French trimmed

For the port sauce
Splash olive oil
1 shallot, finely chopped
300ml port
300ml beef stock
1 knob butter

For the gingered leeks
2 tablespoons olive oil
Half a leek, cut into 1cm squares and washed
1 small knob fresh root ginger, chopped
1 knob butter

To serve
Mashed potato
Shredded leeks, deep-fried in vegetable oil (180°c) until lightly golden

METHOD

1. In a food processor, blend together the thyme, rosemary, garlic, salt and pepper. Rub the mixture all over the rack of lamb.

2. Heat the oil in a small frying pan and seal the lamb fat side down until golden. Place on a tray and roast in an oven at 180°c for 12 minutes. This will leave the meat cooked pink – cook longer if you prefer it more well done. Once cooked, leave to rest for 5 minutes.

3. For the port sauce, heat the olive oil and fry the chopped shallots. Cook for 2-3 minutes until softened. Pour in the port and reduce by half, then add the beef stock and reduce again. Stir in the butter and season to taste.

4. For the gingered leeks, heat the olive oil in a pan and fry the leeks for 3-4 minutes until softened. Add the ginger and butter and season to taste.

5. When ready to serve, take the rested lamb and slice into 6 cutlets. Place some mashed potato on individual plates, add the leeks and arrange the lamb cutlets finish with the deep-fried leeks and a generous spoonful of the port sauce.

"Try this flavour combination and rack of lamb will never be the same again"

" *It's a hit out of Africa, or in it* "

DECADANCE

Desserts are always a talking point at any meal, especially when they can be a bit creative and flamboyant. Well this one hit the big time when I demonstrated it at a food show in Johannesburg. The African media went wild over it so I thought I'd share it with you.

With the use of chocolate transfers you can create something quite spectacular with just a little bit of imagination.

INGREDIENTS *(Serves 10)*

For the base
400g chocolate Hob Nob biscuits – crushed
100g melted butter

For the cheesecake mix
500g mascarpone cream cheese
50g caster sugar
350ml whipping cream, whipped
350g white chocolate, melted

For the topping
75g caster sugar
375ml whipping cream
175g dark chocolate
75g butter

To serve
Pure vanilla ice cream
Multi-coloured chocolate transfer sheets
Seasonal fruits

METHOD

1. For the base, mix together the crushed biscuits and butter. Press into 10 mousse rings laid out on a cling-filmed tray.

2. Gently mix together the mascarpone and sugar, fold in the whipped cream then quickly fold in the melted chocolate. Fill each ring with mixture to just under the rim and smooth out. Refrigerate.

3. For the topping, boil the sugar and cream together and simmer for 8 minutes or until a pale yellow colour, mix in the chocolate and butter, cool slightly then top each cheesecake with the mixture. Leave to set for about 2 hours in the fridge.

4. When ready to serve, remove the cheesecakes from their moulds, place on a plate and finish with the ice cream, chocolate transfer sheets and seasonal fruits.

TRIFLETASTIC!

Once in a while you need a special showcase dessert that creates a certain 'wow!' factor. This has to be the one. A layered trifle extravaganza. A sheer indulgence of chocolate, fruit mousse and custard. Get those long spoons at the ready.

INGREDIENTS *(Serves – A lot!!)*

Quick chocolate mousse
100g hazelnuts, roasted and chopped
200g dark chocolate
600ml whipping cream
70g icing sugar

Mango and white chocolate ganache
200ml whipping cream
200ml mango purée
400g white chocolate
Additional 200ml whipping cream, soft whipped

Raspberry jelly
500ml stock syrup
500ml raspberry coulis
8 leaves gelatine, soaked

Vanilla cream
1000ml whipping cream
235g caster sugar
1 vanilla pod, split half lengthways
4 leaves gelatine, soaked

To serve
Mini chocolate doughnuts
Sponge fingers
Whipped cream
Chocolate sauce
Sugar garnishes
Jam Swiss roll, sliced
Orange jelly

METHOD

For the quick chocolate mousse:

1. Melt the chocolate and add the roasted Hazelnuts.
2. Whip the cream and icing sugar together to form soft peaks.
3. Cool the chocolate mixture to blood temperature then fold in carefully the whipped cream.

For the mango and white mousse ganache:

1. Bring the mango purée and cream to the boil. Add the white chocolate and stir until melted. Leave to cool.
2. Cool the chocolate mixture to blood temperature then carefully fold in the whipped cream.

For the raspberry jelly:

1. Warm the stock syrup and raspberry coulis, add the soaked gelatine and stir until dissolved. Leave to cool then pour and leave to set.

For the vanilla cream:

1. In a pan warm the cream, sugar and vanilla together and bring to the boil. Remove from the heat, stir in the gelatine and leave to infuse. When cool remove the vanilla pod and pour into glass vases and leave to set

To serve:

1. The above are just 4 layers of your trifle. Experiment with your favourite fruit purées and chocolate.
2. Choose the biggest vase you can find, layer up your mousses, jellies and cream. Make sure each layer is set before you add another one. Alternate with doughnuts, sponge fingers and Swiss roll. Get the family involved and enjoy!

WHIPPIE SCRUMPTIOUS FUDGE MALLOW DELIGHT ICE CREAM

Like all great dishes, this one receives a dedication. It was inspired by one of my early food heroes, Willy Wonka. I used to love watching Charlie and the Chocolate Factory with the likes of Veruca Salt and Augustus Gloop. And I also enthused about Wonka's latest creation, the Whippie Scrumptious Fudge Mallow Delight Bar. What else could I do? Voila, Whippie Scrumptious Fudge Mallow Delight Ice Cream. When I served it at the restaurant I even accompanied it with an edible marzipan Umper Lumper. Now all we need is a golden ticket...

INGREDIENTS

400ml milk
100ml whipping cream
1 vanilla pod, split
4 egg yolks
100g caster sugar
25g dark chocolate
2 Whippie Scrumptious Fudge Mallow Delight bars, roughly chopped. If you can't find these, substitute with your favourite chocolate bar

To finish
Dark chocolate transfer cylinders (available from Nutters Restaurant)

METHOD

1. Warm the milk, cream and vanilla together and bring to a light simmer. Remove from the heat and leave to infuse for 20 minutes.

2. Mix together the egg yolks and sugar. Remove the vanilla pod from the milk mixture and re-boil. Pour half the milk mixture onto the eggs and mix well, then return the mixture back to the milk in the pan.

3. Return the pan to the stove and place over a gentle heat, stirring all the time, until it coats the back of a spoon. Remove from the heat and pass through a sieve.

4. Stir in the chocolate and leave to cool, stirring occasionally until it is cool enough to place in the fridge.

5. When you are ready to freeze the ice cream, place in an ice-cream maker and follow the guidelines for your particular machine to freeze and churn. Just before removing from the machine add the chopped Wonka bars and stir through. Place in the freezer for 30 minutes to firm.

6. When ready to serve, scoop generous portions and decorate with the dark chocolate cylinders.

B KEEPERS DELIGHT

You'll get a buzz out of this quirky honey-themed dessert, which combines crunchy honeycomb, chocolate and ice cream.

INGREDIENTS

For the honeycomb
See Page 180

For the ice cream balls
500ml your favourite ice cream
200g dark chocolate, melted and cooked to blood temperature
200g white chocolate, melted and cooked to blood temperature

To serve
Chocolate cone
Chocolate B

METHOD

1. To make the cone, line a cream horn mould with greaseproof paper. Brush with melted chocolate then leave to set. Repeat with another layer of chocolate and leave to set again.

2. To make the chocolate B – copy the outline of the B onto greaseproof paper, pipe neatly with dark, white and orange chocolate and leave to set.

3. For the ice cream balls, take a parisienne scoop and scoop out balls of ice cream, placing them onto a chilled baking sheet. Return to freezer for 20 minutes to harden.

4. Take the cooled chocolate and dip each ice cream ball into either the dark or white chocolate – place back onto the baking sheet and return to freezer until ready to use.

5. When you are ready to amuse your friends, peel off the greaseproof paper from the chocolate cone. Arrange on a plate, scatter around the ice cream balls, the honeycomb and finally decorate with your chocolate B – Buzz Buzz.

CINDERELLA SHOE

W hen love is in the air and cherries are in the shops, all juicy and plump, make this as the ultimate ending for any romantic dinner. Just watch out for the stones. Choking on them is a bit of a passion-killer.

INGREDIENTS

800g fresh black cherries with the stalks on
200g dark chocolate
200g white chocolate
100g orange chocolate

To serve
1 chocolate shoe (a mould for domestic use can be bought from the Home Chocolate Factory or any good specialist chocolate supplies shop)
Few edible diamond sugar crystals

METHOD

1. Wash the cherries and pat dry with a cloth (any moisture will affect the chocolate).
2. Melt the chocolates separately in a bowl over a pan of simmering water.
3. Take each cherry and dip into the chocolates – placing them on a tray lined with food wrap – leave to set.
4. If you want a two-tone effect, take the cherries once set and dip half way into a contrasting colour chocolate and again leave to set, or splash with the coloured chocolate and swirl with a cocktail stick.
5. Once set – trim the top of each cherry – place in petit four cases and serve. Alternatively create the ultimate wow factor and serve cascading from a chocolate shoe with edible diamonds!

nUTS! ABOUT MY SUPPLIERS

BIRTWISTLE BUTCHERS – MEAT AND GAME

A 4th generation family butchers, they supply me the finest meat around, much of it locally-sourced. This includes their Harefield beef and lamb which is melt-in-the-mouth tender, the beautiful Tatton venison and Harrison's home-reared poussins. Matthew is always there to help out and he's a great mate as well.

REG "GOOSNARGH" JOHNSON – JOHNSON & SWARBRICK

The king of poultry. Supplier to the restaurant of farm-reared ducks, chicken and on Christmas Day, corn-fed turkey. So down to earth, he's most definitely put Goosnargh (a little village near Preston) on the map.

C & G NEVE – FISH MERCHANTS

From the beginning, when I met Chris Neve on a flight back from Belfast with the North West Culinary Circle,
I have never needed to look around to find another fish company. The quality of the fish they catch, source and supply is second to none and it makes my job so easy working with great produce.

The boys in their office are always there for a laugh and a good few drinks. Back in the old days, when a certain Nigel manned the phones, he took me to Fleetwood's finest – The Jolly Sailor. But let's not mention the stripping incident which was later reported in the Sunday Sport.

Now Nez, Steve and Andy are the voices at the other end of the line. I'll get a call at 1.00am as to what is due to be landed that morning and it's on my doorstep by 7.00am. That's fresh for you.

PETER PAPRILL – "THE CHEESE DETECTIVE"

One of the great characters of the North-West food scene. He sources all the finest cheeses for me, focusing on small producers and great artisan cheeses. Notebook in hand, he's always there if you need any advice.

PETER SCHOFIELD – DAIRY

For over 17 years, Peter has supplied us with milk, cream and as we go to print, a total of 775,200 eggs. That would make an awfully big omelette. Peter is always there, day and night in case of any emergencies. And keeps us up to date with the village gossip.

R.NOONE AND SON – FRUIT AND VEGETABLES

I used to get up at 4am each morning scouring Manchester's Smithfield Market for any fruit and vegetable bargains – great at the time, but a bit tiring as I'd only had a few hours sleep.

One morning at 10am there was a knock on the restaurant door. A young (well youngish), well-dressed lady stood before me, clutching a whole tray of fantastic English berries and fruits, a whole kaleidoscope of colours. The kitchen gave a roar of approval and thumbs up, not only for the fruit but also on how short her skirt was!! This was Maggie, Michael's wife, touting for business and it worked. Talk about getting your foot in the door. And I got to get my lie-in and beauty sleep each morning.

Mike and Maggie Noone are a great family business. Even their daughters help out. They really do care and will drop anything to help out. They source me all my fruit and vegetables and come to me first with any new finding on the market. They also buy great Christmas presents!

METRIC CONVERSION CHART

WEIGHT

Metric	Imperial
15 g	½ oz
20 g	¾ oz
25 g	1 oz
35 g	1¼ oz
40 g	1½ oz
50 g	1¾ oz
55 g	2 oz
60 g	2¼ oz
70 g	2½ oz
75 g	2¾ oz
85 g	3 oz
90 g	3¼ oz
100 g	3½ oz
115 g	4 oz
125 g	4½ oz
140 g	5 oz
150 g	5½ oz
175 g	6 oz
190 g	6½ oz
200 g	7 oz
215 g	7½ oz
225 g	8 oz
240 g	8½ oz
250 g	9 oz
275 g	9½ oz
280 g	10 oz
300 g	10½ oz
315 g	11 oz
325 g	11½ oz
350 g	12 oz
365 g	12½ oz
375 g	13 oz
400 g	14 oz
425 g	15 oz
450 g	1 lb
500 g	1 lb 2 oz
550 g	1 lb 4 oz
600 g	1 lb 5 oz
650 g	1 lb 7 oz
700 g	1 lb 9 oz
750 g	1 lb 10 oz
800 g	1 lb 12 oz
850 g	1 lb 14 oz
900 g	2 lb
955 g	2 lb 2 oz
1 kg	2 lb 4 oz
1.25 kg	2 lb 12 oz
1.3 kg	3 lb
1.5 kg	3 lb 5 oz
1.6 kg	3 lb 8 oz
1.82 kg	4 lb
2 kg	4 lb 8oz
2.25 kg	5 lb
2.5 kg	5 lb 8 oz
2.7 kg	6 lb
3 kg	6 lb 8 oz

VOLUME

Metric	Imperial
15 ml	½ fl oz
30 ml	1 fl oz
50 ml	2 fl oz
75 ml	2½ fl oz
100 ml	3½ fl oz
125 ml	4 fl oz
150 ml	5 fl oz / ¼ pint
175 ml	6 fl oz
200 ml	7 fl oz / ⅓ pint
225 ml	8 fl oz
250 ml	9 fl oz
300 ml	10 fl oz / ½ pint
350 ml	12 fl oz
400 ml	14 fl oz
425 ml	15 fl oz / ¾ pint
450 ml	16 fl oz
500 ml	18 fl oz
600 ml	20 fl oz / 1 pint
568 ml	1 pint milk
700 ml	1¼ pint
850 ml	1½ pint
1 litre	1¾ pint
1.2 litres	2 pint
1.3 litres	2¼ pint
1.4 litres	2½ pint
1.5 litres	2¾ pint
1.7 litres	3 pint
2 litres	3½ pint
2.5 litres	4½ pint
2.8 litres	5 pint
3 litres	5¼ pint

SPOONS

Metric	Imperial
1.25 ml	¼ tsp
2.5 ml	½ tsp
5 ml	1 tsp
10 ml	2 tsp
15 ml	1 tbsp / 3 tsp
30 ml	2 tbsp
45 ml	3 tbsp
60 ml	4 tbsp
75 ml	5 tbsp
90 ml	6 tbsp

LINEAR

Metric	Imperial
2 mm	1/16 in
3 mm	⅛ in
5 mm	¼ in
8 mm	⅜ in
10 mm / 1 cm	½ in
15 mm	⅝ in
2 cm	¾ in
2.5 cm	1 in
3 cm	1¼ in
4 cm	1½ in
4.5 cm	1¾ in
5 cm	2 in
5.5 cm	2¼ in
6 cm	2½ in
7 cm	2¾ in
7.5 cm	3 in
8.5 cm	3¼ in
9 cm	3½ in
9.5 cm	3¾ in
10 cm	4 in
11 cm	4¼ in
12 cm	4½ in
13 cm	5 in
14 cm	5½ in
15 cm	6 in
16 cm	6¼ in
17 cm	6½ in
18 cm	7 in
19 cm	7½ in
20 cm	8 in
22 cm	8½ in
23 cm	9 in
24 cm	9½ in
25 cm	10 in
26 cm	10½ in
27 cm	10¾ in
28 cm	11 in
29 cm	11½ in
30 cm	12 in
31 cm	12¼ in
33 cm	13 in
34 cm	13½ in
35 cm	13¾ in
37 cm	14½ in
38 cm	15 in
39 cm	15¼ in
40 cm	16 in
42 cm	16½ in
43 cm	17 in
44 cm	17½ in
46 cm	18 in
48 cm	19 in
50 cm	20 in